Warning!

This book contains language that some readers
could find offensive. We would respectfully suggest
that those who might be so offended do not read
any further.

Printed and published in Scotland by Famedram Publishers Limited

Bloody Casuals

Diary of a Football Hooligan

JAY ALLAN

Northern Books from *Famedram*

Acknowledgements

I SHOULD like to thank Jakki for typing the book and for magic support when I was in jail, including fifty letters. Also my lovely sister Susie for the amazing number of hours put in typing a draft and correcting my terrible spelling.

I couldn't have managed without the encouragement of my father and him getting a publisher when I had given up hope. And I would like to thank Bill Williams for having the courage to publish this book when others hadn't the bottle to go for it.

Thanks, mum, for allowing it to be published.

JAY ALLAN
Tenerife, 1989

Contents

Jay Allan, 1989

Preface

THE SCREW whose parting words to me were said with such sneering confidence really did me a favour. He told me that, like all the young cons who said they were going straight out of jail, I would be back for sure. And this book was written as part of the process of proving him wrong. I had to relive it all in detail and write it down plainly to get rid of it. But more than that, I didn't want to walk away without pointing out that, although there were cases of vandalism and of innocent people getting involved, that wasn't what we were about. As far as we were concerned we wanted the other side's Casuals and nobody else was worth bothering about.

Considering I'm not used to sitting down and thinking and writing it was surprisingly easy to get the words flowing. It was almost as good as the real thing writing away in the little room in my parents' house overlooking the peaceful Ythan Valley. Often I'd break into a sweat and feel my heart going like an engine.

The plan was to get me out of Aberdeen and away from the temptations and the challenges to violence and away from the hating police who thought I should have got two years whereas I only had to serve two months inside. I was to work on the farm helping my father prepare his cattle for a big sale he was planning. But even in those peaceful surroundings the image of the hard-man was hard to shake off.

One of my regular jobs was to feed six pure Simmental bulls each weighing three-quarters of a tonne. I gave them a mixture of bran, flake maize, sugar beet pulp and fishmeal. We call that *mash*. Anyway me and Jakki were having a quiet drink with my

7

sister and brother-in-law when I remembered that I had to feed the bulls last thing. "I'll have to mash the bulls when we get home." I said to Jakki.

"Oh, no Jay" she cried, "please dinna hurt them."

But sometimes my training as a Casual has come in handy. Like when there is trouble in the bar which I run in Tenerife. I have about a dozen good looking boys who act as waiters, barmen, bouncers and DJs and they mostly cut their teeth on the football terraces of old Britain. They are OK when the fighting starts but they can't handle the squaring up and the mouthing bit. I don't mind it as they usually back off and if it does come to blows there are soon so many in it it doesn't matter if you are overmatched one-to-one.

Anyway, one of the lads, Warren, came to me and complained that he'd been shouldered and told to "Fuckin' watch it, you posing bastard." Warren knew I'd have a go and said it was "that big bastard dancing there." I waited till he went back to where he and his five mates were sitting.

With all the scene boys waiting for me to start it I walked up and squared up to all six foot three of him. "You startin' on one of my mates, pal?"

"What?" A look of disgust and disbelief was on the big lad's face.

"You fuckin' heard."

Just then I got a tug at my shoulder. It was Stuart. "No Jay not him, HIM" he pointed to another big lad in a group some fifteen yards away.

"Sorry mate, I thought you were somebody else."

But it was too late, the big lad was all fired up by this time. "What the fuck were you going to say anyway?" he said with definite violence in his voice. He looked round to his mates and when they nodded their support he started pushing my shoulder.

Nothing I said made any difference and with all my boys watching I had no choice but bash a crashing head into his teeth. All his mates jumped up for the battle but couldn't believe how quickly it was all over as scene boys came at them across the tables and the seats.

Fair's fair, so after the demolition I ran over to the original offender, smacked his face and threw him out.

So you see, though it went badly wrong in that case, I no longer go in for what my father would call mindless violence. I often walk away, (after all stitches are so expensive in Spain) and only use violence to keep order.

A lot has happened to me since the days as a Casual. The most memorable including the weekends fishing up the West Coast of Scotland with some other ex-trendies. Setting off with Greg to discover the bits of Europe we missed out on the football trips. Armed with a book called *Working Abroad in Winter*, our Euro-Rail cards and our rucksacks took us to Amsterdam where they sell sex in shop windows and grass in every café and we even got to Nairobi where, when we entered Bubbles Disco we were met with squeals of "Fresh Meat!" from the girls. We got our first jobs washing dishes in the Austrian ski resort of Kitzbühel, moved to selling tickets for disco tours on the beaches of Majorca and finally to the Paradise Lost Bar in Tenerife. But that's another story ...

Foreword

Norman Bonney, Lecturer in Sociology,
University of Aberdeen

MANY READERS will justifiably find most of this book offensive. It is full of foul language and approving accounts of physical harm inflicted upon the police and supporters of rival football teams. It relates the adventures of a gang which developed out of a much larger group of more orderly behaved supporters of Aberdeen Football Club in the early and middle 1980s. This first hand account by one of the leading figures in the gang portrays a social circle where adolescents and some older persons in their late teens and early twenties gain excitement and personal reputations among their peers through collectively participating in violent clashes and adventures surrounding football matches involving their own team. It portrays a social world depicting the worst features of male roles in our society. Excess drinking surrounds most of the episodes related in the volume; the participants take pride in inflicting pain; they maraud around football matches craving a clash with their rivals associated with the opposition football team. "Everyone", writes Jay Allan referring to the gang members "wanted their Saturday ration of violence and excitement".

Accounts of behaviour such as this by those directly involved are rare. However reprehensible the behaviour described may appear to the reader, this book has some redeeming qualities. First this account contributes greatly to the understanding of the disorderly behaviour which is engaged in by a significant and socially troublesome minority of football club supporters. It becomes possible on the basis of this book for others to enter the mind of the football match hooligan and begin to understand from his own perspective what motivates such behaviour. Such an account is thus of value to the general public and to those with a more specialised interest in managing crowd behaviour at football matches. Club officials, safety officers, the police, magistrates, journalists and social scientists will have much to learn from the book.

A second redeeming feature of the book is the moral sting in the tale which should deter anyone who might be motivated to emulate the behaviour described in it. Jay Allan seems to have been unaware as he participated in the events which he re-counts that he and his friends might come to grief as a result of these activities. This is despite a record of offences which becomes apparent towards the end of the book. The values and culture of the gang provided an insulating environment which protected its members from censure from the outside world and encouraged them to continue with the behaviour which it rewarded. Arrest, trial and imprisonment came as a great shock to the offenders. The author vividly recounts the pains of imprisonment and gives an interesting account of life in Craig-inches Jail in Aberdeen including some fascinating contrasts with life on a North Sea oilrig where he usually worked for two weeks each month. The "short, sharp, shock" treatment of three months' imprisonment, commuted to two months for good be-haviour, seems to have worked very appropriately in this case. With a supportive family behind him he has started to recon-struct his life on a more positive basis. Prison does not appear to have damaged him greatly although others might have reacted more negatively to the experience. For people from more disadvantaged backgrounds imprisonment can contrib-ute to a downward spiral in their life course. For Jay Allan it provided an opportunity for reflection and reconstruction and this book is one product of this process.

The Aberdeen Soccer Casuals, as the gang became known, contributed to a new style in football hooliganism distinguished not by skinhead fashions but by the wearing of expensive and trendy sportswear accompanied by a heightened level of vio-lence. They acquired a fearsome reputation. "We were the

11

fearsome and notorious Aberdeen Soccer Casuals and how we loved it". As the author notes, they generated considerable embarrassment for Aberdeen Football Club which generally had, and continues to have, a reputation as one of the best run football clubs in Great Britain. Since the jailing of the Aberdeen offenders Scotland has generally been spared the worst of the spectator hooliganism which has sullied the reputation of English football in more recent years. It is ironic that the Casual style was exported to England and last appeared north of the Border in May 1989 amongst the entourage of English fans at the Scotland-England game at Hampden Park.

The marauding adventures of the Aberdeen Soccer Casuals recounted in this volume tell much about the psychology and social structuring of occasional disorder and violence at football matches. Away trips attract particular excitement for the participants. The clashes with rival teams' fans are premeditated in that they are the main purpose of the adventure. The actual match itself is a secondary event. The police appear generally skilled in managing the large crowds and avoiding many potential confrontations, but inevitably determined gangs intent on battle secure their objective in usually isolated and fringe settings away from the stadium and main transport channels. The attitudes, behaviour and characteristics of the Casuals closely resemble those of street gangs in urban situations which have been reported and analysed in many countries. The members are young males in their teens and early twenties. They are age graded. In this case the cadets are the "under fives" i.e. those not of drinking age. There is the emphasis on dress as a form of group differentiation and a concern with collective group reputation. Individuals too earn a reputation for special feats of bravado, aggression or informal leadership. As with other forms of gang fighting, and indeed with warfare generally, aggression is not uncontrolled but is governed by conceptions of what is appropriate behaviour in the conflict situation. When in London to attend a game between two English teams the Aberdeen Casuals are not regarded by the other two groups of supporters or themselves as appropriate participants in the hostilities. Weapons are not favoured, although occasionally bottles and stones are thrown. "Putting the boot in", kicking a man several times when he's down is a favoured means of attack. The death of a victim, which nearly happened in the case of an Hibernian supporter, is clearly not desired.

"Nobody, at least nobody I know, wants to kill. It's just a game. A few stitches, a few scars, fair enough – but death – that's a different story."

The main difference between the behaviour reported in this book and conventional street gangs is that there is no fixed "turf", but rather a mobile one surrounding the football team itself. In past decades poverty restricted the mobility of street gang members to certain urban neighbourhoods. Nowadays higher income levels allow some hooligan gangs to travel more widely. The Casuals and their corresponding peers associated with other teams are essentially gangs which have attached themselves to the football clubs usually deriving from their home community.

Jay Allan's account of his experience with the Aberdeen Casuals will usefully feed into the public debate about the vexed issue of controlling troublesome crowd behaviour at football matches. The account triggers in my mind a response similar to that evoked by earlier studies of gang behaviour. How can the energy and motivation of the gang members be more constructively channelled both in the interests of the hooligans themselves and the general public? There are signs in the account of incipient group organisation among the gang members e.g.: collecting subscriptions and organising bus outings to away matches, as again has been noted in many studies of street gangs. Should not the clubs themselves, or supporters' associations, contribute to the fostering of such tendencies and play a much more active role in organising and leading supporters' activities? They could facilitate their supporters' attendance at away matches and help provide a programme of activities for supporters in the home town. Constructive leadership at this level might provide the vehicle for encouraging more responsible behaviour by the wayward minority of football fans. Football club management must extend beyond team management and running a stadium safely if British soccer is to attain a more acceptable level of fan behaviour. Clubs which

13

fail in their responsibilities in this regard might be threatened with withdrawal of their FA status or other penalties. If clubs and supporter's associations don't take a lead in such matters there will be increasing public pressure for government intervention as is already evident with the government's plans for compulsory membership schemes in England.

Introduction

THIS BOOK is written in the close season of 1986. It's about football hooliganism in Britain – in particular, the emergence of organised groups of youths called 'Casuals' or 'Trendies' or 'Scally vags'. They emerged around 1980/81 and, although they are quieter now due to a massive police crack-down and the use of jail sentences since the Heysel disaster in Brussels, where 38 people were tragically killed, and the Millwall-Luton riot, where hundreds of fans tore Luton ground apart and fought with police, they are still going strong in almost every city in Britain.

This book is not in any way written to glorify hooliganism or Aberdeen's hooligans. Having been an Aberdeen Casual for four years, having travelled to England and Europe with other Casuals, and having served a jail sentence for my part in an ambush of visiting Casuals, I feel that I have stories and views that would be of great interest to many people. It's for ordinary folk that I write.

All the events described did happen at some time, though possibly not all on the day I mentioned. Not all of the names are real. Some of the lads prefer not to be mentioned, possibly because they are still Casuals, but most of those who are included here are no longer taking part.

The book contains some vulgar language – it can be offensive, but it's the way the Casuals speak.

CHAPTER 1

A Particularly Violent Day

EIGHT AM at the Schooner Bar, Aberdeen. A young lad, Ray, joins three others who are waiting for the bar to open: Jim, Mole and Strath. He is told, as all the others will be, that twenty five have already left Aberdeen on the 7am train – some to check out the shops in Glasgow for a new jumper or jacket, and some who simply couldn't sleep for sheer excitement and anticipation of the day ahead. You leave on the first train and come home on the last, if you've got the bottle.

A heavy key turns in the door and the four walk in, shampooed, shaved, with gold chains on their necks and about £180 worth of clothes on each. Jim is first at the bar: "What yous for then, boys? Me and Strath's startin' with orange. So's Mole. Ray?"

"Ah, make it a pint of lager and lime, seein' as it's Celtic."

They all laugh. On days like this it's always tough, especially after the match, and that's they way they like it. Jim has a bottle of Pils for good measure.

With vintage UB40 playing, the boys grab a table slowly, in ones and twos. More trendies enter the bar. Many have had very little sleep, but they don't care. It's Celtic today and they've been speaking about it for weeks.

By 8.25am there are around thirty-five in the bar, mostly discussing rubble in the town last night or what they're wearing, or the possibilities of rubble at Scottish and English games. Usually some Aberdeen boys travel to England but not on the big ones – and Celtic certainly is a big one. A couple of lads from Torry are meeting two lads from Leeds, and there's always a few Scallies from Liverpool, but never more than ten. They can

16

come with Aberdeen as long as there's not too many of them – because it's Aberdeen's mob, not Aberdeen plus somebody.

8.35am. Now there's about 60 in the bar. One large group round a small table is the nucleus of the mob, an unwritten but accepted fact. There are about 25 of the elite, and even within that there is a scale of rank, though not many discuss it. Major decisions like train times, time to leave bars for the match or for rubble, and routes to avoid police, are decided amongst these top boys, and of these lads there are normally no more than two major decision makers, or as some would say, leaders. For two years I was one of the leaders, and to the majority of young Casuals I was the number one, although Ray was always there, too.

"Got any hash?" Jim shouts over to Glennie, who's just walked in. "Lovely little half-quarter of black here, my sons. Don't worry, we'll get wasted on the train."

One of the under-fives is handing out new north east firm stickers. There's around 50 under-fives and more big lads are jumping off buses and taxis, panicking that they won't have time to get their tickets. For different reasons – wages lost at cards or simply because they're out of a job – there are normally one or two, sometimes three, 'tappers', who get 50p or £1 from as many people as they can to pay for the train, food and a couple of pints. I have seen a young tapper clear a card school of £50 from 50ps given to him by those in the school.

As we walk to the platform the usual railway coppers are there, looking for drink. The same half dozen cops – as long as you keep the joints under the table and don't get caught jumping the train, they're alright, not like the real filth in the town. "Well Mr Allan," said one PC, "I see there's a good team of you going today."

"Aye, there'll be a sound when this lot hits Glasgow, I'm nae jokin!"

As the train pulls away at 9.06am there are just over 200 Casuals and around 25 scarfers (or Christmas Trees, as we call them) on board. They are not our enemies – far from it, we've saved their skins a few times. The Casuals and scarfers, however, never go together in the town of an away game. It's not that all scarfers hate fighting, but Christmas Trees usually fight when they lose a game. For us fighting is the game. You get boring games like St Mirren and good games like Celtic. Almost all Celtic and Rangers' fans want to play. They may throw stones and run from us, but they all enjoy the game.

The lads are now settled in. There are fifteen card schools and seven or eight groups of hash smokers. A couple of lads manage to get their half bottles of vodka and orange on, hidden down their balls. Most like to keep control of their senses. Some like to drink what they can to dull the sight of the hundreds behind the handful they might be running into.

I play on the big boys' table while the going is good. The same old faces are there; Watty, Turdie, Gregg, Big D and two more who wait for dropouts. There's always an audience of ten or a dozen, and plenty look-outs to shout when the guard comes on so that one or two jumpers can hide in between the seats. An old favourite of the jumpers is to sit on the bog with your jeans and pants to the floor and leave the door saying 'Vacant', so that any punter will just get embarrassed and go elsewhere, and the guard won't check a vacant bog.

In the school, pots of £30 and £40 are not rare for three card brag. The most I won was on a train to Hibs – £74. When we got to our usual bar in Edinburgh my round was 18 pints of lager, two tops and three lime, 60 fags and four pies. That was a score gone for a start, but it's the accepted thing to do, to stand your hand when you're in the winnings. And quite right, too.

Another ten Casuals come on at Stonehaven, and a handful at Montrose, but from then on you're no longer in your manor. Now you're entering jute territory. Many good rucks have been had in Dundee, but it's harder now because, as in Aberdeen, the police are very well organised, and there are so many when you play Dundee, or Dundee United, there's always the same faces. It's not so much one football team against another (although at games of high importance it can make confrontations even more violent), it's more one city against another.

The next stop is Perth, home of St Johnstone. Although they have a small, violent mob, they're a bit primitive – still skinheads – and there aren't that many of them.

Stirling is half an hour from Glasgow and sometimes some of the younger lads (the under-5s) get off here. That's because if it's an early train then all the big boys go for beers and the under-5s are left alone on the streets of Glasgow. If there are too few on an early train then they'll just get off and wait for the next train, and more under-5s for back-up.

Once past Stirling, the adrenalin really starts to flow. The lads get restless and the card schools stop. Tension is high, not through fear (at least not generally) but through overwhelming excitement and anticipation. For sure there will be the usual police presence, sneering down their noses at us. "Scum," they'll say, and we'll look at them just long enough not to get pulled up. Even some of the coppers are recognisable from previous games. How feverishly hated they are – hated more than the lads we've travelled to fight.

There will also be representatives of other mobs there to suss out how many are coming off this train. Maybe Rangers or Motherwell will be there, waiting for a train to Edinburgh, or a couple of West Ham ICF or Scouse Scallies just up for the day to see what this Aberdeen mob is like. They'll have read about the mob in *The Face* or *The Maker,* or seen it in a real paper like *The Observer* . However, I think even football thugs, while realising that all the fashion and violence is real, know that stories about us in gutter press newspapers are glorified beyond all recognition.

The corridors of the train are full now, and the doorways are solid. The time is 12.30pm and everyone wants to be on the platform first. Your boat at the front of the mob, that's the business.

As the train slows down to stop, Casuals are filing out of the train, bursting with excitement. We're in Glasgow once again – magic! We wonder what's going to happen this time, and hope it's as mental as Rangers was earlier this season.

The scene is pretty much standard. There's about 20 uniformed cops in the building, and quite a few vans just outside. (It's a funny thing that coppers are supposed to be such heroes for stopping violence, when sometimes I think they love it more than we do. Nothing pleases them more than dragging a young thug by the hair into their van, knees in his ribs and kicking him in the legs or back. They always make sure they don't hit your face and let you sue them. I have witnessed a cop with a Hearts scarf outside Tynecastle shouting: "Come on then, you Casual bastards", and when the Casual he was challenging booted him in the legs, he whisked him off into a nearby car and charged him with police assault. There's got to be something wrong there, surely.)

As usual, Paul and a couple of mates (Aberdeen Casuals from Glasgow) are amongst the welcoming party which includes two lads from Edinburgh, seven from Fife, the 25 that travelled on the 7am train, 16 boozy Hazelhead Casuals from a minibus and three cars-full whose drivers just had to show the lads their new motors.

All in all, there's just short of 300 of the best boys. There will be a couple of hundred more on the specials, mainly younger boys, but this is our service crew. We are told immediately that three under-5s got done by Motherwell (the Saturday Service) on their way to play Hibs in Edinburgh. It's quite common for small groups to get rucked when they're looking around the shops.

Three Scousers, Liverpool Scallies, are the only English spies today. We don't mind them looking on 'cause they'll tell their lads back home how Aberdeen's got a good big firm and they're all mental.

The police start walking towards us and the lads don't even bother with all the bullshit. "If you want to see the game move along now!" It's time to head into town anyway.

Whenever your mob gets off a train, out of a bar or out of the ground it always looks so much bigger. I don't know exactly why it is, but walking in a mob of 200 or more is a fantastic feeling – it's probably the security and the feeling of power. It's also magic watching all the amazement on the public's face, the pointing fingers. I think most of them realise it's not them we want to harm. The punter out walking and shopping is no target, the days of running down streets with shaved heads, braces and DM's, smashing house windows is past. I wonder what they got out of that.

No. What the modern thug wants is to fight his opposite number in different areas and cities from his own. They want to fight us. We want to fight them. I've even seen thugs from Aberdeen witness for an opposition Casual in Edinburgh and vice versa. I think they just know that when it's down to courts it's them against us, no matter which city you're from.

Everyone heads for one of three or so bars that are big enough to hold the bulk of the lads. Today it's beside Central Station. It's well situated, has plenty of room and a good juke box. When we get about twenty-five yards from the bar some of the boys start running, making sure they get their whistle wet before the rest of the lads. Bottled Becks is the order of the day – tastes great and doesn't bloat you up like pints of lager or beer. Also, they're easy to carry through mobs of youths queuing to get served, or easily popped into your jacket to be drunk in the street or even thrown at opposition Casuals that you can't catch. We seldom throw things. Hand-to-hand combat is much more fun than throwing bottles and stones at each other. Glasgow has been famous for years for its running stone fights, and heavy bottles of Irn Bru are a definite favourite with the locals.

It's 12.45pm now and most are on their third bottle. There are about 180 in the Central Bar and around 40 in Tropics round the corner. There's more chance of a go when there's fewer of you.

Just before 1pm, Finlay comes up to our table and reports that two of our under-5s just got wasted outside Austin Reed's and one of them is away to hospital. Some of the lads have already gone looking for the bastards. Suddenly someone runs in and shouts: "Celtic's outside, c'mon". There's a huge rush to the door, the bar staff watch in amazement as the lads bottle-neck, swaying and pushing, dying to get out and into them. It's a bit of a disappointment when we get into the street to find there's only about 40 Celtic, and as soon as our under-5s know the lads are behind them they steam into Celtic. They don't stand long. As we make our way back inside a white cop van pulls up. Shit! That's all we need. Now they know where we are for sure, and they'll keep tabs on us till we're off their patch. That's the best thing about Glasgow – you can be walking in an escort and suddenly you're on your own again. They don't give a shit if there's trouble, just as long as it's not on their manor.

1.15pm now, and the suggestions start over when we should leave for the match. The eager lads say 1.30pm; the boozers say

Aberdeen F.C., Pride of Scotland.

Hibs
Hearts
Dundee
Rangers
United
Celtic

The Casuals Never run.

2.30pm. 2.15pm is decided by me, Ray and Big D.

By 1.30pm some of the lads are feeling the drink, and confidence is high. One of the top lads, Flakes, says with a laugh: "Look around boys! What a fuckin' mob we've got, we're gonna waste Celtic, we're gonna fuckin' kill them!".

"C'mon then boys, it's a quarter past, let's go, let's go do it," Ray says. I look at my watch – 2.15pm. I take a last long swig of my Becks and the whole bar starts swilling large gulps down their throats. A couple of boys look really pissed off – they've just paid for pints. But when the top lads go, everyone goes.

Passers-by stop and stare as more and more and more youths file out of the bar like a Paul Daniels hanky trick. I always think: "Jesus, no way were we all in one pub". We're joined by nearly 100 under-5s, the lads from Tropics and quite a few late comers off the football special train. All in all there are around 350-400 of us. The sun is shining and all the lads are smiling. This is what we live for; this is what life is all about. I wish this walk to Parkhead would last forever, though I hope we won't just be walking all the way.

We like fighting other teams' Casuals best – that's who we really want. But, especially with the Old Firm, there's thousands who want to fight just like us, but are scarfers and hate even the Casuals of their own team. Aberdeen Casuals must be the most hated group of people in Scotland. We like it that way, it means that more people are willing to have a go.

It always starts the same. Going to Parkhead, some lads start punching the odd face and then the first time there's a decent mob of Celtic together everyone just goes for it non-stop until we get to the ground, and hopefully get a few hooks inside too. (This day turned out to be an exceptionally good one to remember.)

"Fuckin' magic, the cops are off."

"Brilliant. OK boys, let's do it."

"Come on, let's get nearer the front."

Everyone is talking now, everyone knows it's time. There's plenty of Celtic scarfers on their way to the ground.

A corporation bus passes jammed with Celtic (Tims) and on the top deck they're all banging on their windows and shouting, "You're fuckin' dead you Casual bastards."

Just in front of us the bus stopped and to my amazement the shouters got off. Me and Big D were nearest so we didn't hang around, I butted the nearest one to me and Big D hooked another. It was as though a starting gun had been fired. The fifteen or so are joined by 20 more Celtic from a bar and fighting is breaking out everywhere at the front. Every corporation bus that passes is solid with Tims, and the under-5s are doing in their windows. Lots of Celtic get off further up and join the barney.

2.30pm, London Road is a riot. There's a mob behind us getting bigger all the time, and there's a huge mob in front of us. Meanwhile me and 20 others are chasing 30 mods and skinheads up some side road – might as well waste them too. The bastards are too fast, though, and we just manage a punch off one face and a boot in the hip. Two lads kicked some scooters over.

Back in the main street there are unbelievable scenes, typical for Glasgow. It's now a stone and bottle affair – they won't stand and fight. They run up really close, throw their stones and bottles, then run like hell for more arms. At least six or seven shop-keepers run out to put their tin shutters down.

In the buses now Celtic are kicking out their own windows, and throwing anything they can get their hands on, from coins to their Irn Bru bottles. The chaos lasts a good five minutes before the first police van arrives, but the next six vans are very close behind.

At the bottom of the mob, the police grab any they can see still fighting. From experience, most of the lads know to stop when the bill steam in. It's just not worth getting lifted. Having said that, there are a few charged at every game. Some don't see the bill in time, some are too involved in the ruck, and some are too pissed to give a damn.

Russell from Hazelhead, one of the boozers from the minibus, is thrown in the van along with two Celtic scarfers. As vans scream up through the street to the top fight, bodies scatter everywhere and most Aberdeen head along one side road. Two Aberdeen Casuals are lifted, and about five more drunken Celtic fans.

By now just about everyone is together again, and we're in

an escort. Quite a few of the boys are sporting cuts and scuff marks, but everyone is smiling. Jesus! we just ran Celtic from both sides and by the end we were well outnumbered. Everyone talks at once, discussing their part of the action. No doubt, some exaggerate, some lie. But one thing is for sure – Aberdeen Casuals did very well. We showed the bastards, we showed them alright.

Now most of the boys have had a taste, there's nothing will stop them. Everyone is totally psyched up now, ready for anything. "That's us 'till after the game now, boys," says Ray, and we know he's right. There are now seven police on horseback, four vans, and about forty-four foot cops. One way or another, our mob is now about 300 strong – God knows where the rest went. Only around five were lifted. I suppose there were a few who couldn't handle the pressure on London Road and did a shoot. Some may have chased Glasgow boys too far and got lost or wasted. Still, at least three quarters of the boys are still left, and they will run from no-one now.

By 2.45pm we are being escorted through the car park at Parkhead. Some Celtic bears are shouting abuse at the other side of the horses, things like: "Come to the Barras and we'll fucking kill you, by the way," and "Ma wife an' her mates could do yous, ya bastards". All of course said with the usual growl of the Glasgow accent. They speak like dogs bark.

Most of the English are terrified by the Glasgow accent, but although there are a lot of hard areas and hard men in Glasgow, the same could be said of every big city in Britain. Their reputation is definitely exaggerated.

When we get through the turnstiles, we make our way up to the terrace. The Rangers end is segregated; we have half and Celtic the other. There's a large gap in the terrace between sets of fans, heavy barriers and about 100 police trying to keep it that way.

There are already about 200 Casuals at the top of the Aberdeen support. Stories filter through that five of the boys originally with us in London Road split from the mob and got jumped. Rob's hand is cut pretty bad, Bones has got a nasty cut on his cheek, and poor Gab is away to get a glass cut on his hand stitched. When I see Rob's hand I say: "What the hell happened to you then, eh?"

"Oh we got jumped. I'm nae jokin', there was about twenty of them. We stood, though, but they had bottles or glasses clean out of a bar."

2.56pm The players come out to massive roars, and both supports burst into song. The crowd is 43,000; Aberdeen have around 9,000 of them. After kick-off, Aberdeen force a corner straight away. The fans reply with one arm in the air, swaying "Come on ye reds!" All the Casual mob start singing "Ran away, ran away, ran away..." to the Celtic on the other side of the segregation. And for the first time we get a glimpse of the Celtic trendies — a pathetic looking lot. There are only 150-200 of them, and it looks like none of them are even 18. "What a shit mob."

The game is going very well. Midway through the first half, the Dons have the edge in a very tight match. Roy Aitken and Willie Miller are bouncing opposition players all over the park. There's the usual thundrous roar from the jungle every time a decision goes against Celtic. Of course, a lot of the lads are more interested in a slagging match than a football match. Whenever Celtic come out with one of their beloved religious (or anti-religious) songs like *Roamin' in the Gloamin'* or *Soldiers are We*, all the lads wave their hands in the air and conduct the massive orchestra of Glasgwegians with rum on their breath and vodka injected oranges in their pockets. I don't pretend to understand the Catholic/Protestant hatred, or how they slander the Queen and the Pope respectively. As far as I'm concerned both are good, gentle and peace-loving people. Surely neither could properly be described as a bastard?

Most of the Casuals do watch Aberdeen when they play, and do genuinely love the club and players, but for some the only good thing about winning is that you get a good bounce at the goals. Also, it makes the away fans mad, and therefore more willing to come ahead after the game.

The half time whistle goes, me and a few lads go out of the terrace into the back to see if there's any chance of a go. "Who's that skinhead down there eh?" Terry points down to a bonehead beside one of the entrances. "Come on," he says, "let's find out". Terry: "Hey skinhead, who are you?"

Skinhead: "Ah'm no Celtic, I fuckin' hate Celtic".

Tel: "Well you're no Aberdeen with a skinhead, are you".

Bonehead: "Ah'm wantin' to fight wi youz against they Tim bastards".

The skinhead pulls up his jumper to reveal a Union Jack t-shirt, proving at least that he certainly isn't Celtic.

Terry, pissed off with talking, punches him in the mouth and says: "Fuck off, no skins in our mob. We fuckin' hate Rangers anyway". The skinhead doesn't seem too impressed, so Terry runs in again, punches him and boots him until it sinks into the boy that we weren't wanting him to stick around and go for a few beers with us after the game.

Some of the lads managed to get some rubble in the bogs, but apart from that, it was a quiet half time, and now, at 3.56pm, everyone is back on the terrace to watch Celtic kick-off.

Proving how big the influence of the fighting is, I can't remember exactly the score of the match but I know that we won and when our first goal went in it was the usual scene. All the players celebrate, Fergie and Garner jump on to the track, hands in the air. And all the Casuals and scarfers bounce and shout hysterically. The whole Aberdeen sings a deafening "We're gonna win the league", followed by all the Casuals with appropriate hand signals singing "one nil, one nil..." to the tune of *Amazing Grace*.

Aberdeen scored the winner and the Reds are still bouncing on the terrace when a familiar song with a real volume and feeling goes up from the Celtic support: "You're gonna get your fuckin' heads kicked in". To this they receive the usual reply of everyone waving their hands in the air to a high-pitched *woo woo's* or maybe just a round of applause for coming out with such an original song. One thing is for sure, though, there's going to be rubble after this game. There's going to be thousands of mad Celtic, a few hundred who're pissed off at the doing they got on London Road, and about 150 Celtic Casuals. At full time the adrenalin is high. No doubt some are a bit wary and some are a bit scared but for the bulk it's smiles all round – time to steam in again.

Before the game, because people take different forms of transport, drink in different bars or go shopping instead, the mob is never all there. But straight after the game you can see properly how many boys you've got. Today we're pretty impressive. Looking back at all the heads I reckon there must be around 500; certainly no less than 450.

Everyone sticks together now. You're OK with a mob, but leave it and you're in trouble. Heading towards the first street of Celtic supporters, some of the lads are weaving their way to the front with anticipation. Suddenly a stone comes flying towards us, quickly followed by another, and then a half bottle (empty of course). The effect of this is like the starting gun at the London Marathon; the Casuals wade in in droves. Celtic stand their ground. A really violent flare-up has started, and Celtic are running from everywhere to join the fun.

By the time the police wade in, minutes of mental battles had taken place, and for some time it's a relief – they are totally knackered. Nobody has really won this battle. A few of us got hit; a few of them got hit, the best thing is that there's been a good battle and, when outnumbered, the lads stood no problem. Two more of the boozy Hazelhead lot got lifted, and a couple of Tims were thrown in the van as well.

That's the good thing about Celtic and Rangers – when they lose the match they do go mental. And because there are so many of them, you're battling all the way to the station.

Unfortunately, we've picked up a large police escort again, and four or five vans stretch the length of the mob (about 100 yards). There are five or six horses, too. The police have crushed everyone onto the grass verge and pavement at the side of the road, and we take the long way to Queen Street.

Some boys right at the front are striding out as fast as they can go without running, trying to get a fight without being seen by the coppers. There's a mob of about 40 Celtic just in front of them across the road and the usual constant stream of Celtic fans heading for the city centre. Something has to happen soon.

It does. To the great joy of the lads, there's about 100 Celtic Casuals, and we get our chance. Aberdeen stream across the road and there is total panic. Horses are turned where Aberdeen are fighting, and at least two folk are knocked to the ground by them. Another few are arrested. When the police eventually pull Celtic back up the road and settle the Aberdeen lot back to walking, it's clear that that there's little chance of more rubble as the police are greatly reinforced. Nearly 100 police in all are escorting Aberdeen. It's usually possible for small groups to break away from the escort, but the bulk will be escorted all the way to the station now. A few times the mob runs to try to shake the law, but with their radios and vans they make those attempts useless.

Thinking the day is over, quite a lot – over 100 – start to jog to Queen Street Station trying to catch the 5.25pm special back to Aberdeen. Mostly they're the under-5s or the lads with nagging birds. The bulk will take the 6pm service train; a hard-core will wait for the 7.25pm, which unfortunately is the last train to leave Glasgow for Aberdeen.

When we get to Queen Street it's pretty obvious that there'll be no more violence, at least until the police escort is thinned down. About 25 of us go into Samuel Dow's bar, just next to the station. Pints are bought and we all sit down to talk about the day's events. It's been a good day for the Aberdeen Casuals. Came to Glasgow, ran amok, won the match, and still have a chance of some more. With most of the lads packed safely on their way home, Celtic Casuals will get braver and start milling around the station. Also, Rangers have to come back from Paisley, and Motherwell's Casuals will probably go home from Edinburgh via Glasgow.

During the discussion we find out that Watty, Brooner and Arsenal Steve are lifted, along with a dozen lesser-known Casuals. The Scousers we met off the train are now in Dow's with us, and they start educating some of the lads on how to screw bandits – quite easy with a bit of plastic strimmer wire on metal slots or 10p s wrapped in silver paper and put into 50p plastic slots. One of the Scouse Scallies takes Telboy and Glennie to the next-door bar to show them how it's done. With so much unemployment in Liverpool, Scousers are the Kings of fraud. They can fix your electricity meter with a wire or rub off a signature on credit cards with brake fluid and sign their own names. They know the lot, and I suppose with no job and no prospects it's not really surprising.

Twenty minutes later the bandit frauders are back, pockets bulging with 10p pieces. They got £16 in total, and that emptied the machine.

"Anyone knockin' around outside, Tel?"

"Naw, naebody, and there's still heaps of coppers – watching this bar, too. There's no danger of another go now, no chance!"

As we leave Sammy Dow's at 7.15pm it's soon apparent that Terry was right. The bill have sharpened themselves up a bit now, though it's got to be said that they didn't do well today. Quick pop into Casey Jones for a quarter-pounder, and then we get straight on to the train.

It's always annoying that you can't take drink on the train for the way home. Trying to keep you sober on the way down so that you don't fight at the match is fair enough, but when you've been in the bar having a few beers with your mates and you're not going to get home until 10.30pm, it's a bummer not being able to take a couple of cans to ease the boredom of the return journey. This journey is as boring as usual, and some of the lads go to sleep. We're all relieved when it pulls into Aberdeen station. It's 10.35pm. Magic! – there's time to nip up to Tammels to see the second half on the box.

When we get to Tammels, the upstairs lounge is mobbed with Casuals all watching the match, and we manage to see the winning goal and a couple of sways and bounces from our mob in the terrace behind the goal. Most of the lads will stay in the top bar until 1am, but those with suitable clothing to get into discos will do so.

Me, Ged, Clouse, Gregg and a couple of others go to Gabriel's night-club, where there's an excellent sound system, chilled bottled beers, and plenty talent. By the end of the night (2.30am) all of us are well boozy. Ged and Gregg come with me to my flat while Clouse and the other lads make their way to the taxi rank. There are always about 40 or 50 folk hanging around the stance until at least 3am and sometimes 4am. There are always a few girls hanging around, and hundreds of late-night revellers join the queue to get their taxis home. It's a real social centre at weekends. You might well get yourself invited to a party and get laid. Or you can get into a barney with some bikers or drunken mannies who start on you. Worst of all, you can get lifted. The police are never far away – they only get out of sight long enough for a fight to start and then swoop in, hoping for arrests. On a Saturday night pounds are spent on chipping the white paint off their cars, and blue paint off their vans. Not just by Casuals either.

It's 3am when we get home, and it's time for bed, but what a good time we've had. We look forward to Dundee Utd at home next week, but we'll remember today for a long time as a particularly violent day.

CHAPTER 2

Gothenburg

"WE'RE ON the march with Fergie's army, we're all going to Gothenburg..."

We'd been singing it for weeks and weeks, and now at last it really was time to go. The time was 8am, the day, Sunday 8th May 1983, and our journey was to the European Cup Winners' Cup Final in Gothenburg: Aberdeen FC v Real Madrid. Aberdeen had to be taken seriously after knocking out Bayern Munich in the Quarters. People believed Aberdeen could do it. We would soon find out now, anyway.

Unfortunately our mode of transport was a bus. Nobody at the time cared, though. At last our team had reached a European Cup Final. It was not only Casuals on the bus but Weg, Gregg, Jim, Johnboy, Flex, Watty, Beanz, Dave Gregg, Harvey and a few younger Casuals (I don't know their names) were there.

We boarded the 'Parks of Hamilton' bus and were told that we were to pick up more fans in Perth and then move on to the long distance bus at the depot in Hamilton. Just as well, too, there wasn't even a bog on this one, never mind video and reclining seats. Imagine going all the way through Europe to Sweden and back in a bus with no bog. There were around 35 of us on our bus, half Casuals and half 'scarfers'. Only a few had a can or two of lager – it was just a bit too early for most, but the atmosphere was really good. We picked up seven more fans in Perth and made our way to Hamilton. We were looking forward to getting on to the proper bus so that we could relax and settle in.

Some Casuals went in other buses; a few flew from Aberdeen; and some went by train; and some lucky ones went on the St Clair, a ferry that took 500 fans on a "Cruise to Glory". All in all, about 60 Casuals made the trip. You had to feel sorry for all the lads who couldn't make it, but we didn't let that spoil things. For some, it was their first away game in Europe, although many had been to the glorious 0-0 draw in Munich, Germany, and some had even made the trip to Belgium despite Aberdeen thumping them (Waterschie) 5-1 in the first leg at Pittodrie.

When we arrived at the 'Parks of Hamilton' bus depot in Motherwell and Hamilton, everyone eagerly scanned the area for a long distance bus that would be home for the next few days. We all looked in confused disbelief when we parked next to an identical, single-deck bus. The drivers got out and walked on to the next bus. We got out of our original bus and went to find out the score. Weg walked up to the drivers: "If this is our bus to Gothenburg you've got to be jokin', mate".

"Sorry pal, it's written here, this is the bus all right."

"Well you better get us another bus – there's not even a bog on here, how the fuck do you expect us to go all the way to Gothenburg without a bog?"

Arguments flew from drivers to fans.

Driver: "Listen lads, we're no' very happy either. There's no bog for us either you know."

Fans: "Aye, well you're getting paid for this, we've all paid over a hundred notes for this trip".

After phonecalls and heated arguments for about 20 minutes, we parked our pissed-off bodies on to the bus. Another beautiful, double-decker bus with toilets, reclining seats and videos was with our party. Apparently the reason we didn't get a bigger bus was that there weren't enough of us. Still, the big bus was what our shop had advertised, and the big bus was what we had paid our money for. One thing was for sure – "They will hear about this when we get back to Aberdeen."

There was nearly a bus-against-bus riot when the passengers of the double deck bus started complaining about the time we were taking. Curses were thrown: "Just get on your bus for Christ's sake or we'll never get out of Scotland, never mind go to Sweden";

"Swap buses then, you selfish bastards, would you like to go Gothenburg without a bog?"

"Fuck off!"

Finally we got moving, but unrest on the bus was high. To add insult to injury, we found out that one of the females on the bus was 5 months pregnant. Slowly, everyone cooled down and started to cheer up. "So what if it's a shite bus, at least it's going to Gothenburg," someone said.. "Aye, if it was Celtic or Rangers it would be packed work-vans with no windows and a trail of McEwans cans all the way to Dover. Fuck the bus lads, let's make the most of it, lads. Who's wantin' a smoke?"

By late afternoon we had covered quite a few miles, we were well over the border, and were catching up time, bombing down the first part of the M6 to Preston. At about 5pm we stopped at a service station. When I came back from the toilet I saw some of the lads crowding a bandit. A couple more of us were waved over. I looked down to see Weg frantically trying to break into the money box at the bottom – no sophisticated wire or coins with silver paper round them here, just old-fashioned force. 'Crack!' The lock broke. A huge screwdriver was the tool, and it certainly worked. Weg goes to see Spurs a lot, and I think the Yids have been giving him some tips.

It seemed a bit dodgy to do a bandit when there were so many punters around, but no-one was caught and I think the haul was about £25. When we got back on the road there was plenty of talk about how much money would be made from every service station, and the ferry too.

With most of the day gone, beers were on everyone's minds. We asked the drivers where we were going to stop. They were reluctant to stop in a town, preferring a service station. They knew they would have to, though. Preston was the town. It was 8.15pm, and we were told to be back by 10pm.

Everybody piled off the bus and started running towards bars. The first bar tried was solid with blacks – not a white in sight – and it was a large bar, too, so we thought maybe somewhere else would be sensible. We found a smallish but smart bar just down the road. Juke box, pool table – this would do us fine. There were roughly 20 of us, all Casuals, in the bar, and I don't know if I've ever seen drink being swallowed in such quantities so fast, by so many. It was as if we were loading up for a desert trek like camels do.

The bar was quite homely. It was the first time I'd had a drink in Preston, usually we just stopped in the middle of the night for a few hours, changing trains for Manchester or Blackpool. In the night it's a depressingly bleak looking place, but just then it seemed fine, and the locals were friendly enough. Or were they?

At 9.30pm almost everyone was on their fourth or fifth pint and some were drinking shorts as well. The Cup Final spirit was beginning to show at last: "We're on our way to Gothenburg". It's amazing what a few beers can do.

At 9.45pm two young Casuals (I don't know their names, but they were 16 or 17 year-olds) came in saying they'd just been told to get the fuck out of Preston or they were dead. It was blacks who'd made the threat, and one of them had flashed a blade. Crack! – a pool cue was kneed in half. "No blade will mess this number, anyway," said Watty. He gave the other half to Johnboy and they both put them into their jackets. Another cue suffered the same fate and about six beer bottles and a half dozen pool balls were stashed. We'd heard how mean blacks can be with blades, so the heavier tooled up we were the better.

We swayed out of the bar at 10pm exactly. Pints still full or half full were taken from the bar. As we approached the place where all the Dudes were, we noticed a couple running into the club, undoubtedly to tell them that that mob of Jocks were heading their way.

The blacks started to come out in numbers and the lads prepared. This was not a racist fight, not from our point of view anyway. They'd pulled a blade on a couple of our boys, and they'd pay for it. "Pull a blade now, ya bastards," someone shouted. I saw a glint coming from one of the Dudes' hands. There would have been a bloody battle, but to almost everyone's disappointment the old bill flew into action. I've never been too keen on blade battles. One slash from a Stanley or scalpel knife can split your cheek like an arse.

Luckily no-one got lifted, even though most had full or part-full glasses, and other objects that could be offensive weapons.

We got back on our bus at 10.15pm and there was constant singing for the next two hours. Of course with so much beer in our stomachs and more flowing out of cans, our bladders were full and there wasn't a toilet. It was just like the old days on the buses to Scottish games, pissing in cans and emptying them out of the skylight. You've got to be really careful, especially when you're boozy and the bus is rocking around. Many hands would be pissed on, and there'd be no chance of washing them for hours. What a bloody set-up. Never mind, at least the trip was properly under way now.

Luckily, we didn't have to wait too long – some of the ladies and other punters needed to stop so we went into one of those huge service stations on the M6 just after midnight.

We all went upstairs and to our obvious delight there was a whole room lit up with Space Invaders, Galaxium and Bomber machines, and about ten bandits. "Boys, it's a fucking arcade, let's do it! Let's get some of the people's money back that's lost to those robot-fraud bastards". The big screwdriver was put into overdrive. Five machines were opened, about £150 the total haul. Everyone went back to the bus pissing themselves laughing, "Christ, that was easy". Soon everyone settled down, and finally fell asleep.

Kings Cross Station, London – We woke with arched backs, pins and needles in our arms and legs. It was 5am. London is a fantastic place – many trips are made to the Smoke and many good times are had, but not at 5am. Both drivers changed without paying much attention (many were still asleep), and we got going again soon after 5am.

Dover, 7am – We had all slept again on the road from London, but woke with a little more zest now. At least we'd reached Dover. We all got off the bus and were told we had two hours to fill 'cause the ferry left at 9am. We went to one of the cafés for bacon, eggs and tea, and spoke about what we thought we would be doing that night, and in which country.

Weg and Tommy had been away for ages: "Where have yous two been?" asked Swifty. "In the arcade, come and give us a hand – we've got the machine open but there's some punters in now". Eight of us went with the two of them. It was a breakout machine. A couple of the lads played bandit whilst about seven of us crowded round as if we were watching a breakout wizard. Weg had broken the lock on the front of the machine, but had pushed the door back up to look locked when he came for help.

The machine couldn't have been emptied for weeks. Three Aberdeen FC hats, reserved only for European games and Cup Finals, were filled solid with ten pences – quite a good haul except that now it had to be shared ten ways instead of two. When eventually all the 10p s were shared out we had just over £6 each. Not bad going, £60 off one machine.

We boarded the ferry at 9am, our bus and the double-decker – about 120 Aberdeen altogether on the ferry. Duty Free booze was being purchased in large quantities and although it was just after 9am the bar was pretty busy. By the time the coast of France could be seen for the first time, the bar was in full song.

It was a great feeling, driving off that ferry into France. We had all bought some francs on the ferry. There wasn't even a courier or anyone to give us information as to what currency we would need, or how long we would be staying there. We drove out of Calais about 11am.

The first stop wasn't even in France, but in Belgium, at a transport café place. Luckily, with so many passing through Belgium as they travel in Europe, they accept almost all currencies. The bad thing about this, though, is that it's very easy to get ripped off. Your own currency is sterling, you're paying in French francs and getting Belgian currency as change.

People were getting ripped off right, left and centre at the garage beside the café. Some of the lads evened things up a bit, helping themselves to Cornettos and Choc Ices from the fridge.

We were stopped for about an hour. Some played football on the grass; some got badly ripped off with the chicken and chips in the café; and a few had a beer or two in the bar. It was mid afternoon when we left the café. On the bus, Shiner showed the lads his spoils. He had actually shinned up one of the flagpoles and stolen the Union Jack. He also bought a can of black car spray and neatly sprayed *ABERDEEN TRENDIES 1983* on it.

There are so many borders in Central Europe your hand is

never off your passport. Even though you know you've done nothing wrong and your passport is perfect, you always get slight butterflies in the heart when a man with a gun looks at your boat and then your passport.

Enjoying some beautiful scenery, we crossed through out of Belgium into Holland, through Holland to Germany. It was a long drive and we were all glad when we stopped for the night in Hamburg. The time was 11.35pm.

We weren't looking forward to another night on the bus, but we thought we'd go for a few beers first to make it easier. Just as we were set to leave the bus, one of the drivers stood up and said that everyone was to be back by 12 mid-day the next day. He said no-one was allowed to sleep on the bus. There was a barrage of abuse and furious complaints. At first we didn't think they could possibly be serious – we had no warning of this whatsoever. No-one on the bus could speak German; not many had German marks, one lad was only 15, and that lady was five months pregnant, surely they weren't just going to throw us out on to the Hamburg streets at midnight? Shouts went up: "Where the fuck are we supposed to go? Couldn't you have warned us, you pricks? You've got to be jokin', pal!" We decided against battering the bastards – they had to drive us to Gothenburg. Maybe when we got home.

Eventually, and totally pissed off with our situation, we got off the bus with our bags of fresh clothes and toiletries. Jim, Johnboy, Mark, Lowzer, Dave, Harvey, Shiner and Jasper went off themselves to the Reeperbahn red light district, the Soho of Hamburg. Currency with the whores was no problem, they would part their legs for £15 sterling. All of them came across with the fifteen notes and said it was well worth it even if the whores were so sexy that for some it cost about 50p a shaft, it was so quick.

Buying beers in sterling also, they pissed it up until the last club closed at 5.30am. Out in the streets they said everyone was rushing around going to their work. It wasn't worth their while trying to get a sleep now so they found a five-a-side pitch and played football until all the shops opened in the town.

Thomkins and another guy from the bus, Doctor, had had to run through gardens and hide in bushes – police cars were chasing them after they caused scenes in a brothel. Seemingly they had started shouting and swearing, calling the whores *dogs* and shouting: "I wouldn't fucking pish on you, you dirty boots".

Big D and Quinten went to a bar in the Reeperbahn and were approached by a young lady. She asked Big D to buy her a drink. Well, why not? She was beautiful. When D quickly calculated how much her drink cost (about £5), he said, "you're jestin' lady. You want to drink with us, you drink beer with us." They drank most of the night and weren't tempted to part with £15 for a quick bang.

The rest of us, more worried about getting a shower and a bed for the night, went round a few hotels. We came across one hotel and eventually got it sussed that we'd pay £5 sterling each for the night. We were well pleased, and we all had a shower. Just after his shower, Watty threw his old Y-fronts out into the Hamburg street: "Here's some Scottish skids to sniff, you dirty Krauthead whores". They wisped their way down and landed on a wire stretching across the road. "Ah well, at least if the wind doesn't blow you'll have left your mark in Germany Watty."

Through a keyhole, one of the lads was caught flicking porn pages and wanking on the toilet seat. He wasn't allowed to forget that, I can tell you.

We settled down to a card school and crashed around 2am.

No breakfast in the hotel in the morning, but at least we felt fresh. It was only 8am, the weather was fine and we'd heard how good the sports shops were here. Sports gear was very much in fashion at the time, being the end of the season '82/83. Everyone was talking about Fila tracksuits.

About 6 of us went into a huge sports shop. The selection of trainers and sportswear was unbelievable. I didn't have the bottle to steal anything. I knew the intentions of the other lads so I waited outside. I have a see-through face and I didn't want to get the other boys caught. A bag would be held open when no assistants were around and a tracksuit top buried deep into it. The lads were out five minutes later because the attendants were sussing them out. Nobody was caught, however two Fila and one Sergio Tacchini tracksuit tops was the haul – not bad considering they were worth £45-£50 each.

Just outside we met two Tottenham Yids, over for the sole purpose of thieving clothes. We warned them that some of the assistants were getting a bit dodgy in the store we were in. They went off, no doubt to steal as much trendy gear as they could in a few days and then back to London to flog them to their mob.

We got to the bus just after 11am. Most of the folk from our bus were already there. Stories were exchanged, and when we heard of the times the other boys had had the night before we were a bit jealous, but at least we felt fresh and clean. Tonight would be the big one – Tuesday night was our night on the ferry to Gothenburg.

At 12 noon only two passengers hadn't turned up out of the whole bus. They were two of our lads, Gregg and Tommy. By 12.15pm the drivers were getting impatient, as were most of the other fans. "Where the hell are they? Fucking idiots." I spoke to the drivers. They said they would leave at 12.30pm, with or without them. "Listen, you can't leave them here, their fucking passports are on the bus," I said. Tempers flared on the bus again when the engines were started at 12.30pm. Everyone went crazy at the back of the bus, and someone made a massive slash in one of the seats. The driver just had to stop. By 12.45pm even the most optimistic of us had to admit that something had happened to them. The bus pulled away just after 12.50pm. At least they knew they had to be at the ferry dock in Kiel (Germany) by 8pm – we just had to pray they'd make it.

Losing two brought things down amongst the boys. It wasn't as if they'd just been lifted at a match at home, they were stuck in Hamburg with no passport and they had to make it to Gothenburg for the next day. The thought of watching Aberdeen in the European Cup Winners Cup Final in a bar in Hamburg was the pits. We thought something strange must have happened to them. "Christ's sake! we seen them in the hotel this morning."

We arrived in Kiel in the late afternoon and were let out on the town. Rendezvous time was 7pm at the ferryport. We walked around Kiel in groups. Me, Big D, Quinten and a couple of others went into a Bureau de Change to cash in yet more £20 notes for marks and krona. There was a group of beautiful girls in front of us. We tried on a bit of patter and found out that they were going on our ferry that night to Gothenburg. It was pretty obvious they were Swedish because of their blonde good looks. When they told us there were around sixty of them on a school trip from Gothenburg we could hardly believe it. They sure weren't like schoolgirls back home. They told us there was a disco most of the night. We had already paired ourselves up and were about to entice our lovely prizes into a bar to help loosen up their inhibitions when – Bastard! – a teacher came in with yet more lovelies and whisked our girls away. "Never mind lads," someone said, "this ferry looks like the business."

We had a look around some sports shops. Some Aberdeen fans were being the typical away-from-home-Jock-fans, by drinking wine and beer and singing in the streets.

Sex shows were in abundance, and so we went into one. There were about eight of us now, all fancying a couple of beers and a bit of live smut, a bit of smut to get us in the mood for this ferry. The sex club was a flop. Only after we had all bought a beer at a ridiculous price did we find out that the girls didn't come out until 8pm. Instead we had to watch some ugly French tart give a huge black guy a blowjob on a fuzzy screen on the wall. What a turn-off. A couple of grimy old men sat at the bar smoking what smelt like burning horse shit.

Challenges were thrown from person to person about what would happen on the ferry that night. "Nobody's got an excuse the night, boys," was a general challenge met by: "sixty Swedish tarts, I can't believe my luck", "the blonde thing in the Bureau de Change – she's mine for sure", "the blonde one? They were all blonde you fucking idiot!"

Around quarter to seven we left the bar and made our way to the ferryport. When we got close we saw a huge game of football was under way. To everyone's relief, two of those players were Tommy and Gregg.

The story was that they had been caught about 11.30am, just before they left for the bus, stealing a Fila tracksuit. The store detectives kept them in a room until the law came. They explained that they were Scottish, on their way to Gothenburg for the football, and they had no passports. They also told them that to meet the bus again they would have to be in Kiel by 8pm. The police made them empty their pockets of all their money (about £100), gave them a train pass to Kiel and saw them onto the train. The police even gave them a receipt for their fine. Well, they were skint but at least they were back. The lads would see them alright.

We all got our bags from the bus and went to the ferry queue. The Swedish schoolgirls were all there (there were schoolboys in the party too – but they looked like schoolboys). 15, 16, 17 year-old girls are so much more mature than boys that age, and they always go for older, more mature blokes. We fitted that bill pretty well, and I think the girls were as pleased as we were at the prospect of getting a lot closer to each other on the ferry.

We got to our two-man cabins, showered, shaved, changed and out we went. Duty-free bottles of vodka etc were purchased and taken to the bar. Buying coke or lemonade at the bar and topping them up with vodka or Bacardi, a sensible, thrifty thing to do. Also it would help the shyest of the lads to lose any inhibitions before we steamed into those Swedish tarts.

The disco started at 10pm. Everyone was settled down to drinking apart from Big D who was on the Black Jack table in the casino with Gregg. There were four well-decorated Real Madrid fans at the bar. Nobody would even consider hassling them – this was Europe we were in, there were no fighting plans like at home in the UK. No, this was all about pissing it up, trapping as many foreign broads as possible and winning the cup for Aberdeen.

As time went on and beers went down, the disco was livening up. Weg and Quinten had already made a move and were on a table with a couple of Swedes. Me and Swifty decided to make a move. There was a balcony disco, so we thought we'd give it a bash. Upstairs was pretty lively I suppose it was just after 11pm that we went for it.

We split two pretty nice-looking birds who were dancing together. They spoke good English, as all Swedes do. We went to their table and drank and spoke for about 25 minutes. It was obvious they were interested in us so, bored of speaking, I said: "Give us a kiss, then". She said ok, and gave me a mouth-closed peck on the lips. What a waste of time. I leaned over to Swifty, "fuck this, Swifty, mine's a tight little bitch. I'm going to get nothing from her – I'm off".

What a waste of time! I went to check out downstairs again. A few lads were drinking at the bar. I started to have a laugh with Jim and Johnboy, when Big D came swaggering up to the bar: "What's it to be boys? Order them up, drinks are on me". Jim looked at him in surprise, "do a bit of business on the table, eh?"

"You'd better believe it, son, £200 eh! No problem to Big D".

I had just started to walk to the stairs to go back to the better disco when three girls stopped me. Two weren't particularly nice – a bit young – but one must have been 17 or 18, and she would do anytime. "Are you Scottish, boy?"

"Aye, that's me, how did you guess?"

"You are very pretty, yes?" one of the girls said, "well I think so anyway". I looked at the nice one:

"Do you think so?"

"Yes, definitely, you must dance with us later". Jesus this was great, I didn't even have to try here. The three went towards the dance floor. I tapped the last one (the nice one) on the shoulder. As soon as she turned round I steamed my face into hers. There was no fight. Magic – maybe I'd get a bit more action out of this thing.

I took the lass to a table with Quinten, Weg, and now Big D, all already paired up. The girls all knew each other and you could tell from their glances at each other and the conversations in Swedish that they were comparing and discussing their pieces of Scotch beef.

We pissed around, dancing, drinking, singing Aberdeen songs and taking the piss out of the Swedish girls. No doubt they were taking the piss out of us too, but we were all having a ball. It was well after 2am when we heard a really loud "We're the barmy Aberdeen army" from downstairs. We had to join in. Down we went to view the whole bottom dance floor a sea of Aberdeen fans bouncing and singing. We swayed in and joined the mob. After constant pleas from the DJ that we calm down, the mob started to disperse. The boys reclaimed their birds or sniffed around for something new.

By 3.30am things had quietened down a bit, although there was still plenty of people around. Some lads had managed to get a bird back to the two-man cabins. My trap came willingly through into accommodation level, and as I approached my cabin I prayed Flakes (my cabin-mate) would be one of the many still up and about. The bastard was in there, crashed out. I said: "he's pissed, he'll never wake up," but it was no use – she was having none of it. I tried the next two cabins. Both were full, one with two of the lads sleeping and the next with one of the lads having his evil way with one of my bird's mates. We went to a stairway and had a grope around. Fuck this – if I didn't get something sussed soon I'd burst a blood vessel. There was a door on the stairs with 'Authorised Personnel Only' written on it. The most important authority I knew was speaking to me so in I went. I gestured her to come in but the noisy fan machine didn't seem to turn her on much. Eventually she said she would have to go to bed as it was 4am. I watched her walk away and took myself back to the disco area. "What a waste of time."

The disco was over, but there were still plenty of people around. Two pretty nice-looking girls were sitting in a corridor getting chatted up by one of the scarfers, Dave. I sat down and wondered why they hadn't been snapped up already. After nearly an hour of chatting we, me and the boy, sussed they were sharing a cabin. Five minutes later we were sneaking in. Magic! I thought finally my efforts were not to be in vain. I got on the top bunk with the brunette and Dave got the blonde on the bottom. By the slurping noises I guessed Dave was doing alright, but mine was being really frigid. She was shy to let me kiss her. I thought she was just playing hard to get, but she started talking some bullshit about her boyfriend in Gothenburg and the teacher coming to wake them up.

Totally dismayed, I left the cabin. "At least Dave got his hand on the blonde's triangle; I got buggar all. Shit, it had to be old Pamela again, boring, but at least she is always there, reliable and willing anytime." We were to be up at 8am and it was 7am now. By now there were quite a few people getting up and going to the shower room etc. It seemed hardly worth it, but I went to my bunk and fell asleep.

I was shattered when I got up. Thank God I hadn't gone out in Hamburg, too. We said some goodbyes to the girls we were with and joined the queue to get off the ferry and into Customs. When we got out of Customs our bus was waiting. Also as planned, Ray and Dave were there. We were all pleased to see them and they were happy to be in a bit of a mob at last. They had taken the bus to London, a train to Harwich, ferry to the Hook Van Holland, train to Amsterdam, travelled through Hamburg to Copenhagen and eventually to Gothenburg – nearly four days of constant travel, broken only by a half day in Amsterdam.

Amsterdam is the centre of the world of prostitution. They sit in front of windows looking out into the street where the punters walk around viewing the choice. When they get some-one in it's 50 Guilders in the hand (around £12), close the curtains, on with the durex, quick come, and out. Then they sort their hair, open the curtains again and wait for their next £12. What a life, eh? Anyway, Dave had gone for it but Ray kept his money. Apart from that and a few beers in the bars there, their journey had been pretty boring and they were glad to be with the boys. We squeezed them onto our bus and set off for the town. At last we had arrived in Gothenburg.

We were dropped at the ground pretty early and had all day to ourselves. We all stuck pretty much together. For the first couple of hours we just walked around taking in the sights and booting a ball around. Big D and Weg started chatting up these two birds and so we left them to it.

In the centre there were quite a lot of Aberdeen walking around singing and really getting in the mood. We walked up to this bar which was completely solid, and some fans were drinking pints outside because there simply wasn't enough room inside. We struggled our way into the bar. Everyone was singing their heads off and swaying around. We saw a couple of the lads that came by plane and so they joined us. We didn't even attempt to get served at the bar – we all got back into the street to find another bar or an off-licence.

There is at least one bar on every city centre street in Britain, but the Swedish simply aren't a drinking race. Practically no shops sell alcohol and the bar we visited was actually the only bar in Gothenburg. You could get a drink with a meal – but who wanted a meal? When it's Cup Final time all you want is beer with the boys. We were walking around Gothenburg again when we copped our eyes on Big D and Weg in a restaurant with the two birds they met an hour earlier. "Come on everyone, Mooners, come on!" shouted Watty. Immediately around 20 of us were hauling our jeans and pants to our knees, baring our hairy arses to the window they were eating at. The girls covered their mouths and stared at each other; Weg and Big D were pissing themselves laughing. We finished off with a bounce, singing: "We're the barmy Aberdeen army."

Eventually we found a large wine shop in the middle of a huge shopping centre. You couldn't even buy beer, so wine it had to be. Many bottles were purchased and, wine in hand, we walked back outside. Five minutes later the rain started. It never stopped. We made our way back to the market. So many Aberdeen fans had Aberdeen T-shirts or Scotland tops; some had full strips, and at least a hundred had kilts on. All would suffer.

The market was now pretty mobbed, and we noticed that there were a helluva lot of Swedish girls inside now. We soon found out that the schools had a holiday that day. They started to hang around us. Some no doubt fancied some of the lads, some were enjoying practising their English on us. Whichever, we enjoyed the attention and some of them were beautiful.

Me and Ray walked from group to group speaking to the girls. A blind man without a stick would score in here if he had a Scottish accent. We decided to go for it, and when we gave each other the nod of which one we wanted and we asked the two girls to go for something to eat with us. They came and we took them out of the market and into the rain. We found the first doorway of a shut shop and steamed into them. They said they couldn't take us home so, fed up with kissing and squeezing mammaries, we made our way back to the lads.

It was late afternoon when we got back to the lads, and a fair game of soccer was under way. Weg and Big D returned with large grins on their faces, I think maybe they fared better than me and Ray. Still, just about all the lads were together now, and soon we'd be leaving for the match. We went out into the rain and started walking to the Ullevi Stadium.

The rain never stopped, or even lessened, but our spirits were not dampened. We were going to see our team in a European Final and that was the most important thing in the world. Quite a few Gothenburg fans had attached themselves to us and were very friendly. We were friendly back, especially as they had Aberdeen scarves on. There was no doubt the Swedish public were backing the Jocks rather than the Dagos.

We got to the ground around 6.30pm. Aberdeen fans were everywhere, and nobody seemed the least bit bothered about the rain. Once we got inside the ground we realised that the rain had bothered thousands of the Swedish public. Over 30,000 tickets had been sold but just under 18,000 was the final attendance.

Most of them Aberdeen fans – around 12,000 – while Real Madrid had a surprisingly small following of around 3,000. The other 2,000 or so were Swedes who decided to bear the rain to watch the big match.

It was a bit disappointing, watching our team playing the biggest match in their history in front of less than 20,000 fans. But the Aberdeen support at least were in a Cup Final party mood, and nothing barring defeat would spoil our fun. Around the ground there were the usual banners, so favoured with British clubs and international team's supporters. One which caught my eye read: "Doug Rougvie never lets a Dago by".

Once everyone gathered together, there were about 65-70 of us. There is a standing terrace all the way round the stadium, and a one tier sitting stand above that. We were behind one goal, above the terracing, on the stand.

The players came out and everyone went barmy, bouncing and singing. The match kicked off on the soaking pitch.

I will not talk much of the game itself – this is more about the fans than the actual game. Eric Black had a shot blasting off the bar in the first five minutes. When he scored from close in around the 20 minute mark, the ground erupted. Celebrations were still going on when Alex McLeish made an uncharacteristically bad back pass which Santillo of Madrid intercepted and ran towards goal. Leighton inevitably took him down, and the Spaniards scored to make it 1-1, and that was the half-time score.

In the second half Aberdeen were strong, and the fans got right behind their team. Whenever Stielike got the ball all the lads were screaming: "Kill the fucking hippie. Go on Cooper, break his fucking legs!" There were no more goals in the 90 minutes, and so, nervously, everyone awaited extra time.

A Mark McGhee cross and a John Hewitt header made it 2-1. Everyone exploded – we all leapt the fifteen feet down to the standing terrace below and started dancing and hugging everyone in turn. We must have bounced and danced for five minutes non stop.

When the final whistle went, some of us tried to scale the fence, but it was a really high, barbed-wire fence. Hundreds of police in white jackets and big clubs put us off a bit as well. The smiles on our faces were permanent fixtures now. Fergie was being interviewed just in front of us. What a man of brilliance and class! How much admiration we have for that man.

When the players eventually left, we made our way, bouncing and singing out of the ground. Outside there was a fountain, already solid with fans. We Jocks certainly like our fountains. Kiche and a few others went for it – they had hotels and a ferry to go to. Most of our busload didn't bother as we knew how uncomfortable it would be changing on the bus.

On our way back to the bus, me and a couple of others went up to a Madrid supporters' bus, commiserated with some of their fans, shook hands, and exchanged our hats for Real Madrid scarves. I felt a bit sorry for them, but they have had plenty of success in the past; now it was our turn for the limelight.

When we got back to the bus, important discussions were going on. Some of the lads couldn't handle the idea of a long journey home on our shitty bus and were considering sneaking onto the St Clair ferry boat. Certainly there would be a big celebration on the boat. In the end six of the lads decided to go for it: Weg, Gregg, Flakes, Dave, and two others.

The rest of us didn't want to take the risk. At least now there would be more room at the back of our bus. Ray, who came by train, came home on our bus. We got straight on to a ferry, but unfortunately it was not the long ferry to Kiel, but a much shorter one to Denmark.

We had only two hours on this ferry, but we made the most of it. Some bought wine and champagne, but most of us were discussing the game over a few beers in the bar. The disco started after about half an hour.

Somebody from the other bus on our party had a cassette of Aberdeen FC songs and it was handed to the DJ. He put on a different song every 15 minutes or so, and when he did, every fan on the ferry was up, singing and swaying to the music.

There was a school party on this ferry too, not so many beauties as the Swedes, but a couple of them were really nice. Ray, as usual, was game, so the two of us split a couple who were dancing. As soon as the record was finished the lass I was dancing with said: "Would you like some fresh air?" I went outside with her, and she pressed herself against me straight away. Jesus, this was easy – these Danes certainly knew the score. This thing was hot, but it was the same frustrating story – all wound up and no place to do the business.

Back at the disco the party was in full swing and it would have gone on all night had it not been such a short journey. When the disco stopped and people started to gather bags, all the lads were standing on tables, banging the hands off the roof singing: *Oh Flower of Scotland.*

Someone from the bar and a couple of the ferry's crew tried to calm us down, but they were told to "fuck off..."

With carry-outs and non-stop song we waved the Danish birds goodbye, and got on our shitty bus.

We drank and sang for two hours, until the beers were finished, and eventually everyone crashed out. The journey through Europe wasn't much fun – everyone was hung over and sore from an uncomfortable sleep. We stopped at a Belgian café and grabbed something to eat. Someone discovered that a British 5p coin would buy a packet of fags from the machine, so everyone gave their 5ps to the smokers.

There was one strange thing I noticed in the café. The girl that was in the middle of the bus with one fan was now sitting eating with another fan, and the one ate alone, looking really pissed off. This wasn't surprising when I found out what had happened. The guy she was with originally had been her fiancé. He had persuaded her to come, and he had paid her fare. The punter she was with now she only met on the journey, but she had made up her mind that this new guy was the business. God knows why there wasn't a fight; I think the first boy was just too upset and overwhelmed by it all.

The rest of the journey passed with little incident, and even the ferry to Dover was quiet. When we got back to the mainland it was pissing down rain. Everyone was still pretty quiet, just wanting to get home. Thank God we won – what a miserable lot we'd be if we'd lost. It really puts the damper on things when you've got two whole days on a shitty bus after a game. Everyone decided that from now on it'd be the train or the plane.

We changed drivers again in London, and started the long haul to Hamilton. When we got to Hamilton we changed into that identical bus we'd taken from Aberdeen to Hamilton on Sunday. During that journey from Hamilton to Aberdeen, all the bad feeling about the bus was brewing. It was decided that we would all go and demand a refund from the travel agent. Everyone was fuelled up, and we elected a spokesman.

We arrived back in Aberdeen just before 5pm, and apart from those we'd dropped in Perth, everyone marched into the shop.

The poor lassies behind the desk didn't know if it was New York or New Year. Barrages of complaints were hurled at them across the counter until we managed to shut everyone up and let the spokesman speak, and the lassies phone. One cocky assistant said: "Really, gentlemen, there's no need for you all to be here. We have a list of all your names and addresses and we'll investigate and keep you posted."

"No way," one fan replied, "we want some answers. We want to know why we didn't have a bog or a courier, and we want to know now". The woman gave a smile of superiority: "Well, you're not going to be very comfortable, I mean you can't all sit in here". Our own kind of smile spread amongst the lads – we all knew what would happen now. Inevitably, everyone sat on the floor, to the amazement of the assistant, who walked through to an office at the rear of the shop to hide her blushes.

After about half an hour of phonecalls and arguments but no proper answers, we left, having been assured we would all be contacted within the next two weeks. There was no contact, and I'm glad to say that that shop is now closed.

The other lads had failed to get on the St Clair ferry, and eventually were detained by Swedish police. The police obviously wanted rid of the boys, so they were forced to deport them. They all slept in the police museum on Wednesday night. In the morning all of their money was taken (not nearly enough for a fare to GB). The police made up the price and bought them tickets for a direct ferry from Gothenburg to Harwich. The coppers had a good laugh with the lads and even gave them milk and sandwiches etc. for the journey. On the ferry there were a few Aberdeen fans who had chosen to travel that way. The two groups got talking, and at Harwich the scarfers handed over a collection that was taken to give the lads something for food. They got around £40 – a very nice gesture.

From Harwich they jumped a train to London and, again avoiding the guard, then jumped a train to Glasgow and another to Perth. They got a paper train in Perth at 2am on Friday morning, so getting home a lot quicker and more comfortably than the rest of us.

Eventually, then, everyone got home safely. We had a helluva journey, but we had a lot of laughs on the ferries, and we were there when Aberdeen FC won the Cup Winners' Cup (when the competition included England's teams) – that was the main thing.

CHAPTER 3

Trips to England

A LOT of the lads go to England whenever Aberdeen have a bad fixture or a postponed match. My own experience is limited – I just went on the odd occasion for a change, or when Aberdeen was involved. This chapter describes the matches I was at South of the Border.

The first was back in 1980. We had the might of Liverpool in the European Cup. Fever about the game was high and although I was still at school I just skived a couple of days off and booked my place on the bus along with eleven of my mates.

There was a mob of Aberdeen youths then who fought at the football whenever possible, but it was quite small and had neither organisation nor uniform. Red and black Harrington jackets were quite common, but clothes were not really as important as they are today.

We were really excited as we boarded the bus early that Wednesday morning. We stopped at Perth and everyone bought large carry-outs from the supermarket. Cans of lager and bottles of Pomagne were the order of the day, and we settled down to start drinking. We all knew our that our team had an uphill battle after going down 1-0 at Pittodrie. In those days Aberdeen FC was still a bit inexperienced and young, and we were very proud to be following our team to one of the biggest stages in European competitions, Anfield.

At Carlisle our bus pulled into a huge service area. There were already eight coaches parked there, and the place was mobbed with Aberdeen fans using the toilets, eating in the restaurant and playing Invader machines or Bandits. Me and my mate Steve grabbed a bite to eat and then started playing the 'Galaxian'. We must have played the game for about a quarter of an hour and were totally engrossed in it. Just after I had finished my shot again I had a look round. "Oh shit, Steve look! Where is everybody?" Steve looked in amazement – the whole place was deserted. Why the hell didn't we notice, or why didn't someone give us a shout? The 'Galaxian' was out of our minds totally as we panicked and ran out of the building to the Car Park. All but one of our buses had left, and that bus certainly wasn't the one we'd been on. But one thing was for sure – we had to get it. We threw ourselves at their mercy and luckily there were a couple of seats, though they weren't together.

We felt really bitter – why couldn't someone have just given us a shout? But we were especially annoyed because all our booze was on the other bus: twelve cans of lager and four bottles of Pomagne. At least we'd have plenty for the party on the way home, whether we were celebrating or commiserating. They're both good reasons to get pissed.

After a boring journey of the usual anti-English chants ("If you hate the English bastards clap your hands") we arrived in Liverpool. Steve, who was sitting at the back of the bus, had particularly disliked the journey, being English himself.

Another bad thing about our bus swap was that my ticket was in my bag on the original bus. Luckily I managed to buy a ticket outside the ground, but when I got inside I soon realised that I was in with Scousers. We hassled a copper to put us into the visiting end, and they obliged.

Once in the ground, I saw the lads from our bus. One of them, Gary, was out of his head with drink. No wonder, he'd helped himself to me and Steve's stash. He was good enough to leave four cans. Me and Steve cracked up, "Why the hell didn't someone give us a shout, you better be joking about our booze", the answers we got were "We couldn't find you, we did shout, we thought you must have been lifted or something". Couldn't find us – we were playing the bloody bandit, man! After a few minutes of bitter words the episode was forgotten and the occasion took over.

Aberdeen were crammed into the small section of the Anfield Road end of the stadium, segregated by a four-foot sheet metal wall. They also had a small corner of the Kemlyn Road stand, about 4,000 fans in total. It didn't seem that many, but it was a sight more than the miserable 600 they brought up north. We were in the ground about 20 minutes before the kick-off, and Aberdeen were in full voice. Never once was there a gap in the singing, and the volume was overwhelming. Just next to us at the Anfield Road end were about 500 or 600 young lads. None of them had scarves on, and they all had their hair in a side-shade. I didn't know then who they were, but I now know they were the early dressers. Liverpool was one of the first cities to start the soccer trendies boom, and these lads were the Liverpool Scallywags.

Another thing I couldn't understand was that when we sang songs like: "Where's this thing they called the Kop?" (slagging Liverpool because we were out-singing them) they would return our song with "The Kop's an abortion", showing that Liverpool had not one set of supporters but two, the scarfers in the terrace behind the opposite goal (the 'Kop') and the Scallies in the Anfield Road end.

One song which caused a violent reaction was these Scally-wags chanting alternately: "Celtic, Rangers, Celtic, Rangers". There was an angry sway against the metal wall. The coppers walked up and down the wall thumping everyone with batons. Gary, far too drunk to know any better, started shouting at the coppers and trying to get over the wall into them. He was frogmarched away, as was Cowie, leaving ten out of our original twelve.

After a lively enough start in which Mark McGhee had a brilliant chance saved, spirits were high, but Liverpool eventually took charge and they beat us easily, 4-0. After the game we stayed in the ground, singing and chanting for Fergie "We shall not be moved!" We must have sung for twenty-five minutes, and I really think he should have, but Fergie did not appear.

When we got off the ground the mounted police were waiting. They were escorting us down the road to our buses when some Aberdeen men in front of us started whistling the tune of "Robin Hood, Robin Hood, riding through the glen". One copper on a huge horse moved through the fans right up to the offenders. In his scouse accent he said: "I bet you wouldn't do that to my face, you heroes". Immediately, about ten or a dozen men sang or shouted at the top of their voices, and clapping their hands above their heads: "Robin Hood, Robin Hood, riding through the glen, Robin Hood, Robin Hood, with his band of men..." The copper was helpless, and a more lost looking face I have never seen.

Steve, who was a skinhead at the time, was chatting up two skinhead birds outside the bus. He grabbed their phone number and joined us on the bus. The journey home was long and uncomfortable, and altogether wasn't much of a trip. From the beginning, London has always been favourite. London is fantastic. You can buy any make of garment you like; the sports and clothes shops are excellent. To keep up with the fashion you'd really need to make three or more trips a year. All true trendies well know the taste of the thick toast and tea you get early in the morning in the Kings Cross buffet.

The places we visit usually include old favourites such as Allenell, Lillywhites, Nicknacke, Cecil Gees, Aquascutum and Wood House. Kings Road and Oxford Street are the business. From the punks at Sloane Square to the mods in Carnaby Street, there are endless sights to see.

In 1982 I went to my first all-English encounter. Another brilliant thing about London is that you have so many games to choose from. My mate Steve, who used to follow Arsenal when he lived in the smoke, made sure we chose Highbury.

We had a few beers and talked to some Gooners in the Gunner's bar. Just after 2pm there was the sound of a charge. A few Arsenal ran out of the bar to get into it. We walked outside and I saw about 50 Casuals running from about 100. We went to the corner of the street and watched. Some of the fifty who were running tried to cram into the bar. Glasses were thrown and smashed, showering the bottlenecked crowd. Police intervened before it got too serious. We later learned that the Gooners were doing the chasing; the Scousers the running.

Both mobs were dressed the same: in cagoules and tracksuit tops, with jeans and trainers. They were dressed just like Aberdeen. I wondered at the time how they could tell the difference between each other. Because we were the first by a long way to turn trendy, we're still the only dressers in Scotland

and our enemies were easily recognised: denims and DM's, skinheads and parkas.

We didn't see any more trouble, and so went back for another beer and then into the Clock end of the ground. I was amazed that they actually sold pints of beer in the ground. They certainly couldn't do that in Scotland – I can just imagine what a licensed Celtic/Rangers match would be like. The lager was expensive and watered down so we only had the one. After a disappointing game which ended all square we went for the tube. We had asked inside the ground where the best chance of seeing some more trouble would be, but we were disappointed.

Back at Kings Cross you could see what a huge operation the police had on their hands, keeping all the different mobs apart. Leeds were playing in London and at about 5.30pm they came into Kings Cross station from the Underground tubes. They came up and asked us who we were. When we told them we were Aberdeen we got the usual reaction – not violence, just an interest in what violence is like in Scotland.

Much later, at around 7pm, me and Andy were walking back from a Pizza restaurant when we were confronted by two Cockneys. "Where's all your boys then lads?" one asked. Not knowing what was round the corner, I was a bit wary, but Andy just asked: "What boys is this like?" The Cockney was not impressed: "Come on son, where's your boys? Where's all your fuckin boys now?" Time for me to say: "Hey listen, we're Jocks, right, Aberdeen, Scotland." That did the trick: "Oh shit, sorry lads...thought you was some Everton taking a chance... really sorry, mistaken identity, know what I mean?" We talked to the lads for a while and then went back to our own lads in the railbar.

Just after eight we were still there (about a dozen of us) when the door of the bar opened and about fifteen lads walked in. Everybody braced themselves for a go. They came right up to us and for a while a battle seemed inevitable. They asked who we were. When they found out they were obviously a bit disappointed – they were Gooners, and they thought they'd just stumbled on a gold-mine of Scousers.

They sat down and had a drink with us, talking non-stop violence. One of them who looked a bit out of place was a huge

Geordie skinhead. A Gooner told me that he was down in London working and, although he religiously supported Newcastle, he went round with them for a fight. Some drunk bloke of about 50 years old was sitting next to us, and he started talking to the skinhead because he recognised the accent. The skinhead was happy talking to someone with a Geordie accent again, but suddenly his face dropped. He had found out that the man was a Sunderland supporter. For the already drunk skinhead this was too much to bear. The man was a bit too feeble to hit, so he took his anger out on the lamps that were around the bar. He bent about four of them so they faced south instead of north.

One of the barmaids phoned the bill and about ten minutes later two officers entered the bar. They asked everyone who it was, and received a barrage of abuse for an answer. Then they asked the skinhead if it was him. The skinhead told them if they wanted to speak then they'd do it outside. The police agreed, and on the way outside the skinhead said: "And another thing, if you want to talk to me you can take your fucking hat off". To my amazement the police took their hats off. Eventually the officers just left.

The Gooners were going into the city for more beers and invited us to go along. Our train was leaving at 10.20pm so we couldn't go, but Steve could stay at an aunt's house, so he went with them. We found out a few days later that he had gone for a couple of beers with the Gooners and ended up going to see a band called 'The Business in Blue Coat Boy'. He said he was about the only one at the concert with hair and, although he was too drunk to feel it, got quite badly kicked around. He woke up on Sunday morning in a doorway in Dalston.

In 1981 we were drawn against Ipswich Town in the UEFA Cup. I had just started my first ever job that same week and so I couldn't go but a large mob did travel. I got all the stories, the red's had done the business before, during and after the match. They had battered the Ipswich mob and the win they got was a bonus. I was there as everyone was when we put Bobby Robson and Mick Mills in their place, thrashing them 3-1 at Pittodrie. We were to meet Ipswich again in 1983.

The occasion was a testimonial match for George Burley, but

this time only a few of the lads went down. We were beaten 3-0 at football, but all who travelled were happy because Aberdeen fought and didn't get done. I missed that game because of my job on the oilrigs. I got home from my rig on the Monday and the Tuesday was the day to leave for the big one – Martin Buchan testimonial match, Manchester United versus Aberdeen, and the chance to meet the famous red army.

We'd been looking forward to this all summer, and everyone was talking about it. After appearing at Aberdeen Sheriff Court (where I was fined £100 for assault and £50 for breach of the peace) we set off on the train. I had used my family railcard, and it worked out a mere £6 each for six of us. The Manchester United game was on the Wednesday, but we had arranged to take in the Tottenham v Celtic friendly at Parkhead. There were 15 or 16 in the group, and a small mob of about 100 Tottenham. Weg knew some of them through his frequent visits to Whitehart Lane and so we went with them to Central Station after the game. The Celtic fighters hadn't bothered getting a mob together as there were so few Tottenham, but the Londoners (when they realised that) started battling wherever they could. We went into a tube station and the Yids charged along the platform. Quite a few Celtic ran across the track to escape. At Central Station they split in half: some were continuing to Dundee to watch Spurs play there; some were away home to the smoke.

We had a few beers in Glasgow and then took the train to Preston. We arrived at Preston about 2.30pm where we met about 50 lads who came on one train from Aberdeen, through Edinburgh to Glasgow. It seemed like a not bad turnout, as a lot weren't due to leave until the next day. The bummer was that the first train out of Preston was at 6am the next day, to Blackpool. But you can be sure we got it. Quite a few took a later train straight to Manchester, but we favoured Blackpool. Once there, eight of us went off on our own.

It was so early when we arrived that nothing much was happening. For a place so lively during the afternoon and night, it seemed pretty quiet and dour at 8am. We found a swimming pool and waited the half hour until it opened. We went in and hired trunks and towels. We had to pay a deposit and sign for them, so everyone signed a different Aberdeen football player. I was quite chuffed to sign Alex Ferguson. We had an excellent swim in the quiet pool, enjoying the usual diving and racing. After the swim, shampoo and shower, we set off towards the beach front. We jumped on a tram and headed for the funfair. Most of us had been to Blackpool before. In the summer it's just so full of talent you don't even need to try to get one-night stands – they go for you. I suppose it's because thousands of young lassies and young women are away from their boyfriends or husbands and are dying to get into some other bloke's pants. Almost everyone is available in discos, it's a case of drink and be merry, and screw as much as you can. A place to do the business is no problem either, it's just "your hotel or mine?"

Of course it's not surprising that Blackpool is like this. I mean, there's not many sights to see, not any culture to feast your eyes on, just bright lights, booze, dancing and sex. And many want more.

We had a good time on the rides and stuffing our faces with goodies. After dinner time we headed back towards the station – it was time to hit a bar. We found one pretty close to the station and started having beers, playing pool and darts, and talking about the prospects of rubble at the game. The few beers led to a few more beers and then a session of shorts as the bar was nearing closing time. We all left the bar drunk, and bought a couple of six-packs from an off-licence just next to the station. Everyone was in a brilliant mood on the train. None of us could wait to get to Manchester to see the rest of the lads.

Me and Weg tried our hand with two birds who seemed to be hovering around us. It's amazing what a few beers can do for your confidence. We squeezed and rubbed and kissed what we could before they got off a stop before Manchester. We were polishing off the beers before Manchester when Beanz pushed a burning fag into my arm, just for fun. It didn't really bother me at the time, but I had a mark there for two years after.

When we got to the station we saw the expected sight of Aberdeen Under-5s hanging around all over the station. We learned that a couple of the lads nearly got done by some blacks in the Arndale Centre.

I don't know what they were doing there, but I spoke to a

couple of Chelsea trendies for a while before going into the railbar to see the rest of the lads. Once in the bar, we were an impressive sight. All the top boys were there, all the solid lads you could trust, the ones that never run.

Jim and Peter had nipped over to Leeds to see a few lads they knew. They'd been to a few Leeds games 'cause there's always trouble at them. They described in great detail the Leeds-Chelsea match at Stamford Bridge that ended the 83/84 season. On the Friday night they took a bus from Aberdeen to Leeds arriving at 3am so that the lads had to sleep in the waiting room till morning. When it opened they moved to the buffet, and from there to the bar. Leeds started to appear here and there. All the bars around the place were eventually solid with Leeds Service Crew. Everyone knew to get the 12.15pm to Kings Cross, and they boarded the train in their hundreds. It was supposed to be a day train – no alcohol allowed by law – but despite police being on the train they all had carry-outs and drank them in front of the policemen's noses. The train was packed with around 400 of the Service Crew. There were some Sheffield Wednesday fans at Doncaster station and about forty lads ran off the train and battered them against a wall. The police did nothing.

They arrived at Kings Cross at 2.15pm to find a line of police stretching from their platform right to their tube. Once in the tunnels leading to the tubes, the Leeds had a go with the bill, swaying into them, punching and kicking if they could get off with it. As they struggled with the police the popular song was: "One Arthur Scargill, there's only one Arthur Scargill". They sang anything to do with Yorkshire just to wind the Cockney bill up.

Two or three empty tubes were laid on by the police and they went without stopping to Fulham Broadway. At the door to get out of the tube station there was a search going on – everyone was getting a good pat down. Some plastic-handled Stanley knives and scalpels were thrown to the deck and kicked away..

By the time they were all out of the station it was after 3pm and the game was on. Walking to the bridge they heard two thunderous roars. When they got in the ground they found Chelsea were up 2-0. Near the end of the game Chelsea really started to celebrate. They were winning 5-0 and had clinched promotion to the big First Division. All round the ground (except from the Leeds end of course) they were doing *Knees up Mother Brown* in typical Cockney fashion.

At full-time hundreds and hundreds of Chelsea invaded the pitch, swamping the players. They were on the pitch for about 20 minutes and Leeds had had enough. The Service Crew started throwing everything they could get their hands on over the fence, and were trying to scale the fence to get into Chelsea.

About half an hour after the game had finished some Leeds started smashing in the electric scoreboard with an iron bar. Chelsea saw the damage being done and went mental. The fence held strong, though, so that most of the fighting was against police. At one stage the police charged into Leeds with batons and were showered by missiles. Leeds were kept in the ground for nearly an hour and then given a massive escort back to Fulham Broadway. The same lines of coppers waited and put the crew back on their train to Leeds. All the way back the Leeds were laughing and joking. They had had a good day: they battled with police and they battled with Chelsea. The 5-0 defeat didn't come into it at all. Their train arrived home at around 9am and Jim and Peter had to wait 'til midnight to get a bus back to Aberdeen. They said it was well worth it.

Back in the railbar in Manchester, the ASC were letting the beer flow freely and a couple of the boys had met birds they were with on holiday in Great Yarmouth. Most talked about clothes, football or violence.

As soon as we got outside the railbar, the Under-5s mobilised themselves. There weren't that many of us, but the sixty of us and the thirty young lads were all boozy, experienced and fearless. We walked through the streets towards Old Trafford and although we got heaps of funny looks, no mob, in fact no person, confronted us. This was a big disappointment; we supposed that the Manchester United boys didn't expect us.

When we got to the ground we were searched. One lad had a screwdriver taken off him and another a chisel – and they weren't arrested. Surely the bill didn't believe the story that they were joiners who had set off for the game straight from work.

Inside the ground there were about four hundred scarfers

and a few trendies who'd got lost. During the whole 90 minutes we had a slagging match with Manchester United. There was a huge segregating gap in the terracing between us but we could see they had a good few hundred boys.

At one stage Manchester United were 2-0 up but Peter Weir scored twice to end the game level. Everyone left the ground absolutely choking for a fight. We all kept quiet, trying to avoid an escort. There was a lot of movement as everybody tried to be on the outside of the mob to get the best of the action.

As we walked down the streets all we could ever see were small groups of young Manc's in side streets, always keeping their distance. There were a few coppers with us, but not too many. If only the mob would come we could get stuck right into them.

When there were about 30-40 on a side road watching us, we made a move. We were tearing up the road after them but it was no use – they were too fast. After this we really did get a big escort. We never got a chance to have a pop at the red army.

About ten minutes walk from the ground we were herded against a large wall. A double decker bus had been emptied by police a few hundred yards back. I suppose they just had to wait for the next bus. The police, fed up of walking us and taking all the abuse we could muster, were to cram us all onto this bus. Without paying, of course, everyone eventually squeezed in. There were no less than 100 boys on board and the bus was rocking. We all sang and bounced all the way to the station. A few Manchester United came down to the station, but ran away, and we never did get a good battle like we'd expected. Although we enjoyed the trip, it did seem a helluva long way to go without even getting a decent fight.

In December 1984 the weather was terrible in Scotland, and many games were being affected. One week Aberdeen's game was ruled out on the Thursday, and Ferguson went on his phone straight away to try and fix up a friendly in England. Unfortunately, he came up with a rather unglamorous tie against Fourth division Aldershot. We had already planned to go to London that Saturday and didn't realise how close Aldershot was until we were in London itself.

Sixteen of us caught the Nightrider train from Aberdeen,

£20 one-way. We were to meet Sutly and Ray who had had a few days' holiday in Paris, and the two of them were there when our train arrived in London at 8am. We did our usual scout of the shops and those who could afford to bought clothes or trainers.

After the shopping we went back to Kings Cross, put our stuff into left luggage, checked the times of the trains to Aldershot and then went into the bar for some beers. Before we got onto the train we all bought a few cans and someone bought some cider – we thought we might as well make a party of it seeing as it was such a stupid game we were going to. The journey only took about 45 minutes and we were all forcing lager down our necks, bloated and burping, but enjoying ourselves. When we got off the train we thought we had travelled ten years back in time: skinheads were everywhere. We soon sussed out that this was an army training town, and that the skinheads were soldiers.

We got to the tiny ground and paid ourselves in. The programme was just a folded sheet of paper, but we all bought one anyway. The Aberdeen were warming up on the pitch and a lot of Aldershot youngsters were running on to the pitch getting autographs from the Aberdeen stars. We all jumped the low wall and walked on to the pitch. We spoke to some of the players who recognised us. Eric Black, who was giving Jim Leighton saving practice, stopped doing so to speak to me. He was amazed and proud that we had travelled so far to see them. Some of the other lads spoke to Doug Rougvie and Alex McLeish.

When the players went back inside we started a kick-around at the goal mouth. After five minutes of kicking around a uniformed groundsman came on to the pitch and asked for the ball. It was Ray who had the ball and when he passed it to another lad standing right in front of the groundsman everyone knew what to do. The groundsman ran from one lad to the next, as we calmly stroked the ball around. He was going mad, and had the additional frustration of the 3,500 crowd, for every time the ball was passed a very obvious roar came from the terraces. Eventually we gave him the ball and walked across the pitch to our end of the ground.

There were a few other Aberdeen fans there, maybe fifty or

so, but there wasn't really a mob of Aldershot boys at all. We were a bit disappointed about this because we'd heard that they had had a good go with Blackpool. We guessed that the reason they hadn't turned up was that they just didn't expect any boys to travel from Aberdeen.

The game was unexciting and ended in a 4-1 win, ending Aldershot's 12 month run without home defeat. Not much to be proud of really, since in comparison they are such a small outfit. We walked back to the station, hoping and praying that they'd have a team of boys waiting for us somewhere on the road. No such luck.

When we got back to London we went to Euston Station, famous for trouble since so many mobs travel through it and there are always many hanging round. Before taking the elevator into the station we split up into three or four groups. When we reached the top all eyes were on us. There was a couple of blacks just at the top, a few boys at the café, some at the phones or just scattered around. We hadn't done our split-up job very well, and were sussed out straight away. The boys that were so excellently spread through the station came together so fast, and were all of a sudden right next to us. We braced ourselves for the fight, but the police had noticed the sudden movement and moved between the two groups. Ray spotted a Scouser we knew and started talking to him. He told us that this other mob were QPR, and that although most of them were young lads of 17 or 18, a lot of them carried scalpels.

The police asked us who we were and when we told them we were Aberdeen they escorted us out of Euston and down towards Kings Cross. We stopped in a bar not far from the station and settled down for a drink. We were speaking to some Arsenal scarfers who seemed surprisingly friendly considering they claimed to have been battered after the friendly match in Aberdeen the previous year.

There was a service train at 7.30pm and about half of the lads went to get it. Eight of us decided to stay for a few beers and take the 10.20pm Nightrider home. The other lads would be home earlier, but you could usually get a better sleep on the Nightrider. The reason most of the other lads got the service train was that they'd have time to prepare themselves for their

Sunday league matches in Aberdeen.

We had a few more beers in the Rising Sun, a bar by the station, and then made our way down to the station. We picked up our left luggage and sat down, bags at our feet, for more beer in the rail bar. We discussed our day and everyone agreed it had been a magic trip, just lacking a good fight. A good solid battle would have been the icing on the cake.

Just after 10pm we left with our bags and a few cans for the train A couple of lads were already on the train and I was about to board. I looked behind me and saw Johnboy having an argument across the barrier down beside the front of the train. I saw him drop his bag and challenge. That was enough – and I dropped my bag and ran down the platform, closely followed by four of the lads. I found a gap in the barrier and ran through it. The argument was now hot. Johnboy, Jim and three others were on the other side, and I looked on from the same side as the eight. I soon heard that they were Peterborough lads, but they didn't seem to notice me. Jim must have got fed up with arguing, and I saw him kick through a gap in the barrier so I ran in onto them, smashing one of them on the side of the face. I was immediately thumped to the ground, and felt the boots homing in. Not for long though, just two seconds or so and I could hear thumps but not feel them. Magic! – I knew the boys wouldn't be long. Just a few more seconds and all the foe were off me. I got to my feet and saw Johnboy, just next to me, fending off two of the English, so I steamed into one of them. All six of us were battling hard. Unfortunately and unknown to us, Harvey was getting a bit of a kicking about 20 yards away. I managed to get a few good connections on the face of the boy I was fighting and soon he backed off. I was just about to see how the rest of the boys were doing when I heard someone shout "Watch Jay!" I turned round and smash, a running punch in my face and down I went.

I hadn't expected it and got up immediately, angry and dying for revenge. Mob-against-mob scuffles started and Aberdeen were beginning to do most of the hitting. Peterborough were backing off. "Come to Peterborough, we'll fucking kill you, you Scottish bastards," one of them shouted. Just as we were away to call it a day anyway the coppers came running. We could see them from a distance, though, and had time to grab our gear and run on to the train.

We were all so excited and proud of ourselves that we must have spoken about the five minutes of fighting for two hours. The cake was now iced, and Aldershot is still talked of often, definitely one of our better trips south of the Border.

On Sunday, August 12th 1984, two car-loads of us set off for Leicester, who were having some kind of centenary celebration at Filbert Street, with Aberdeen the opposition for the match.

We stopped just north of Stonehaven for a case of lager and then got on the long drive drinking, laughing, speaking and listening to the sounds from the speakers. Every time there's a trip to England excitement is high, and this was no exception. Seemingly, Leicester had really come up in the world and had a mental mob that gave everyone a run for their money. We hoped to find that true.

After a long, tiring journey with practically no sleep, we arrived in Leicester. It was only 7am. We parked the cars in a car park and went in search of breakfast. After a bite to eat we were walking up the main street again towards the station, and bumped into another car load. We all went up to the station where the rest of the lads were due off the train at 9am. About forty came off the train, a bit disappointing but at least we had a few boys now. It was decided that we'd all meet at the bar at 11am for beers and so everyone split into small groups.

Me, Ray, Kiche and Mark went for a wander. I was trying to find a laundrette to wash a stain from my Ellesse T-shirt, but I couldn't find one anywhere. When we got to the outdoor market we could feel the stares burning into us. We were obviously trendies, with Trib Trab, New Balance, and Diadora trainers, Lacoste, Ellesse, Tacchini, Kappa shorts and T-shirts, and a couple of Giorgio Armani jumpers tied round the neck. One bloke, with a black eye and an Ellesse T-shirt, jeans and trainers, was obviously sussing us out. He came up to us and asked if we were Aberdeen. We said yes. Evil stares were coming from everywhere and we braced ourselves for a battle (most probably a losing one). I probably speak for the other three too, but certainly I was shitting myself.

We walked up the road with the guy, wary as hell, but no-one followed. The Leicester boy was trying hard to find out how many boys we were taking down. He was being friendly, but obviously was very excited at the prospect of a battle that night. He told us quite matter-of-factly that if we wanted rubble we should go to the seats.

We were quite chuffed, back in the bar beside the station. Jim and a few others had come through from Blackpool – they always make the most of away trips, taking a week for a game whenever possible. The bar eventually opened at 11 am and the boys settled down for beers, pool and music. By 12 midday most of the boys were there and just after 12 another carload arrived from Aberdeen. Slowly but surely, our mob was growing.

After the wariness of the morning, the beers were taking over and our confidence grew. The whole bar was talking non stop violence, and the drink ran freely.

Because of the crazy licensing laws in England, and to the great disappointment of all the lads, the bar closed, and we slowly left the premises. There was a bakery close by, and a few of the lads were sitting on the windowsill eating sandwiches and cakes they'd bought there. The baker came out of the shop and told the lads not to sit on his windowsill. He was promptly told to "fuck off", and when he kicked up a ridiculous fuss one of the boys, Ali, walked over to a metal bin, picked up the lid by the handle and smashed the whole front window of the bakery. Police swooped in and he was charged with vandalism. A couple of months later he had to go to Leicester court where he was fined £200, but luckily that was on a Thursday morning so he took in Leicester at home on the Wednesday night.

We knew of a big park a few hundred yards away so we made our way up there, stopping at an off licence for carry-outs. When we got to the park someone was sent back to town to buy a football. There were about 65-70 of us altogether, and a huge soccer match got under way. It was sort of a mixture between football and wrestling – so often the ball was forgotten as another running battle started. They were friendly fights, but the kicks and punches weren't much softer than full force. The only rules really were no kicking in the face or the balls, and no headbutting.

Having failed to get my Ellesse T-shirt washed, I had

borrowed a spare Kappa T-shirt from Kiche. This turned out to be a mistake, as it was ripped to bits during one of me and Ray's many one-to-ones. That little mistake cost me £25 compensation.

When 5pm was approaching and the carryouts were drunk, we all started to leave the park and head for the opening bars. We didn't walk too far, settling for a bar just a couple of hundred yards from the park. It was perfect, and just big enough to hold all the lads. Battle plans were getting under way now, many were wanting to go into the centre right now and "smash the bastards in the market". Unfortunately, though, the police already knew of our presence and reputation, and wouldn't let us into the centre. With about forty minutes to kick-off we all boozily left the bar, dying for a fight. To our great disappointment the police were upon us immediately, in numbers we could hardly believe. We had intended to march through the town in search of a battle but the police (a good fifty of them) took us some long, boring back roads to Filbert Street. We didn't even see anyone 'till we got to the ground, and when there we were bunged straight into our segregated terrace.

We found out that hundreds of picketline police had been drafted in (for this was the time of the miners' strike). The coppers were treating this job like a military operation.

Just before kick-off we saw a scuffle in the seats at the other side of the ground. Three boys were put onto the track by police. As they walked round the track towards us we saw Jim. They'd managed to break the escort somewhere along the line. God knows how he does it, but if there's a fight you can be sure that Jim and his boys are in there somewhere. We all sang the boys' names individually, and then sang a "we're proud of you" song.

During the whole game we had a singing, slagging match. The game was a bit boring and ended in a 1-1 draw. We left the ground hoping for action but, as expected, the police were waiting for us. We were escorted up the road by the biggest ratio of police-to-fans I have ever seen. Leicester boys were sussing us out from bridges and side roads but we couldn't get to them and they couldn't get to us.

As we got further from the ground the escort got slightly smaller. When we got to the station the bulk of Casuals went in, but we told the police of our cars. We spotted about 30 boys homing in on us, and for a moment there were no police between them and us. We took the chance.

Every one of us sprinted down the road towards the oncoming Leicester but, to our great dismay, they started backing off. The boys from the back of their mob pushed up, and it looked like they were going to stand and fight, but the police spoilt things again, getting there just in time. There were no more chances – we were put in our cars and that was that. We drove around the streets for a while, but couldn't find anyone. Eventually we gave up, and dejectedly went home.

Apart from Scotland at Wembley the only other game I went to in England was Newcastle against Chelsea at St James' Park. We didn't get tickets because they don't sell them on the day of the match – presumably to put Chelsea fans off travelling without a ticket, but the ground was a long way off capacity. We heard that there was trouble, including the stabbing of two Cockneys before the game, but we didn't see any. We saw the Chelsea escort an hour after full-time and it was very impressive – about 400 solid-looking lads. The police kept the eager Geordies back. I could hardly believe the age of some of the men waiting around for a fight – some looked as old as forty.

After all the Londoners had left and we had spoken to young Newcastle trendies we left for Edinburgh for a night out. Four of us paid a hotel for a room with four bunk beds and a double in it. All nine of us crashed in it that night. We all trooped out one after the other, in the morning, to the amazement of the landlord, and we paid a blind ear to the shouting demands for more money. We drove off with a one-finger sign – what was he fussing about, he got £24 for one lousy room for the night.

DUFC - DFC
UTILITY
CREW

'STYLE OF 85'

CHAPTER 4

Memorable Moments

AS A Casual I've experienced so many memorable moments and so many fights that this chapter is written to describe a small pick of the best ones which would not have made a whole chapter, described separately.

In the season 1984/85 we travelled in good numbers to one of our more promising encounters, Hibs and Easter Road. For years there has been good solid fighting before and after Hibs games in Edinburgh. Usually we get an early train, drink in Rose Street bars and then make our way to Easter Road just after 2pm via the St James' Shopping Centre. We usually meet some opposition in the centre and I clearly remember a running battle in the tunnel two years previous when a skinhead started swinging around a chain with a small spiked metal ball on the end. Uchter (one of the top boys at the time) got a nasty gash in the back of his head.

On this Saturday there were 350-400 of us and it was a miserable, rainy day. We had a couple of beers and then set off for the match. We hadn't managed to get a fight yet – probably the rain had put a damper on people's aggression. We were nearly in London Road when people in cars started shouting out of their windows that the game was off, and after the fourth or fifth confirmation we turned round and headed into town in disgust. Thank God I had brought a brolly – it was really raining now.

We went back to Waverley Station and were seriously considering what to do. It was suggested that we go to a

Motherwell game, or that we go to Dundee for a match. Nobody wanted to go home, everyone wanted their Saturday ration of violence and excitement. To everyone's sheer delight, Hibs made an appearance. They ran in the side entrance, which is a bridge over the southbound track. All they did was shout a few mouthfuls of abuse and then ran away as the police, who were in the station in large numbers at the time, all ran to the bottom of the stairs to the bridge. We turned from the bridge and charged out of the main entrance, and when we got out of the station, Hibs' boys were just up the road on Princes Street. There were only about 50 of them, but we knew they would grow in numbers. They had got quite a distance in front of us but we kept on running; we ran across Princes Street and down a side street. Soon we realised that our mob had dropped to about 40 boys. Most of the rest had stopped, either because they were knackered or because they were forced to by police on Princes Street and sent back to the station.

Just as it seemed we would lose them we turned a corner to a hail of stones. The Hibs' boys had come over a handy area of road works where they picked up plenty of ammunition, bits of tar and stones. We dodged the stones for a while, but I knew that if we made a move they would run. After a few more stones had landed and there was a small gap I shouted: "Come on then, Reds!" and, face down, ran towards the stone-throwers. With a huge cheer the lads ran right behind me and, as expected, the Hibs dropped their stones and ran. Soon we came on to a larger main road and we could see that Hibs had gathered themselves together and now had about 65 to 85 lads. We were reduced and most of them were younger lads.

I was seriously wondering if we would be wise to go on, not knowing for certain if I could trust all of them to fight till the end when one of the boys came up to me and said: "Come on Jay, everyone is looking to you. If you say go, all of us go." The Hibs were advancing on us now and I felt a burst of loyalty to the ASC. I shouted "Come on then!" and another deafening cheer went up. All of us tore across the road towards Hibs. They turned and ran, every one of them. We never caught them.

Everyone was chuffed – we ran Hibs. But we were disappointed that we never actually got a fight.

Some went home early, but most of the boys stayed in the bars on Rose Street. Being in a different city is a reason to enjoy yourself, and everyone loves being away, though all they do when they are is bum their own city up to everyone, and tell them how brilliant it is to live there.

We got a train around 6pm, all pretty boozy. Some of us wanted to get off in Dundee, but most of the lads by now wanted to get home, fed, and out for the night. About 30 altogether got off at Dundee and most went to Jack Daniel's Bar quite near the station. Feeling invincible for some reason, we went to Castle Street where we know a lot of football lads – Dundee and Dundee United – hang about. We went on to 'Reflections' and got some beer down our necks. The place was full of young people dressed and obviously discoing later on. About 8.30pm we started singing, and we weren't holding anything back: "We are the Aberdeen Soccer Casuals and we fucking hate Dundee." We got heavy stares but, amazingly, nobody was coming up for a go. As we walked out some guy did pull up Paul, and Paul hit him with "If you're worried, you jute bastard, get outside now." The guy backed down, and we walked back to the station. We still had half an hour to wait for our train, so we sat in the rail bar for yet another pint.

I was speaking to four St Mirren fans who'd been watching their team get beat by Dundee United at Tannadice. I looked out of the window to where Paul, who had been chatting up two birds, seemed to be arguing with someone. When I walked out of the door I saw a Dundee Casual dropping his jacket and going for Paul. The Dundee was getting the better of Paul so I ran in and belted him in the face. He turned and ran, and I whacked him a couple more times as he went. Some more Dundee boys came in seconds later, and we got the rest of the boys out of the bar to chase them out. The guy's jacket was still on the deck. It was new, but not up to our standards. Although it would have cost around £40, we offered it to the St Mirren fans, and they snapped it up gladly.

As the train pulled out of Dundee we saw two police officers, one of them with the jacket in his hand, leading the four St Mirren fans into the police box. The St Mirren fans were pleading their innocence and pointing to our train. With a wave and a laugh we moved out of Dundee, to the sound of stones smacking off the train. Still game for action, some of us decided to give Arbroath a go. Only four of us went this time, me, Paul, Munro and Mike.

We went into the first bar we met, and I got the beers in. Four jokers at the bar said: "are you sure you're old enough, boys." We thought we were hearing things, but no, it was true – these four were actually pulling us up. They left the bar and a few seconds later Mike and Paul went out after them. Me and Munro followed shortly and when we got outside we saw the four Arbroath boys getting into our lads. We ran down as fast as we could. I had my brolly with me and I held the top of it and whacked it off one of their heads. I am generally against using weapons 'cause I think it's cowardly, but on this occasion the brolly didn't seem too severe or dangerous a weapon, and it was good fun smacking it off these chocolates' heads. After about a minute they backed off, well beaten, and we went back to finish our beers. When we eventually got back to Aberdeen, we went for an Indian meal before we went off home.

We didn't have long to wait for the postponed game to be played. The match was scheduled for the first Tuesday, pretty bad timing for most people since they'd no notice to give their work that they'd need a half day; no money since they'd just had a weekend with a trip to Edinburgh. We knew our mob would be small, but there was no doubt that we'd be going.

We got the 4pm train and were allowed carryouts on it. Dave had just made it and no more, he had run all the way from his work to the station. We only had about 22 boys but at least we knew that everyone knew what they were letting themselves in for, and were going to make the most of it. One thing for sure – at least there would definitely be many more of them so we'd certainly get a fight.

We got off the train and almost immediately got a sign of things to come. A few stones were thrown from the bridge to the side at Waverley, and then the throwers took off. We took the usual route across Princes Street and down to St James' Centre. We couldn't see much opposition and presumed that most of them thought we weren't coming. We walked out of the centre at the bus depot door and there, to our great joy, were the stone throwers. There were only about six of them and we chased them along the station. So stupidly, two of them ran into the toilets. Me and Mark ran in after them and gave them the works: punch them to the deck and give them three or four hard kicks before moving out quick.

We went on and, just as we turned the corner on to London Road, bumped into a dozen lads about our age, but with scarves on. One of our boys put on a southern Scottish accent and asked "have you seen any of those Aberdeen bastards yet?"

"No that's who we're looking for too."

Nothing else happened on London Road or Easter Road and we turned right to go our usual route to our part of the ground. As we passed a corner before the famous narrow bridge we had to cross, we found about a ton of building bricks. We all knew how outnumbered we would be after the game and so we decided to leave an arsenal of ammunition before the bubble burst on Easter Road. (Fans are always segregated after the game as far as Easter Road where they usually clash) We picked up a couple of bricks and smacked them in half on the pavement kerb. They could do a bit of damage after the match. We got to the ground and saw what we expected – only a few hundred scarfers and about ten southern Aberdeen Casuals. The Hibs fans looked happy to see us – they knew we didn't have enough boys down. We knew we were the top boys, and that we'd give them a helluva run for their money.

After the game we left, tensed up and all ready for anything. A few of the boys, mainly the southerners, simply couldn't face the odds that we were about to face and drifted away from us. There were about 25 of us now, crossing the narrow bridge. All our half bricks were gone when we got to the corner – shit! Someone must have seen them and shifted them.

We were now on the road leading to Easter Road, and though we had no weapons we were still going for it. We could see that Easter Road was absolutely solid, hundreds of fans were moving up it. A lot of those hundreds were just honest football supporters of Hibs, but about 50 yards from Easter Road we saw their boys. With Hibs just turning trendy, they had only about 50 Casuals, but they had about 250 punks, skinheads, and guys just choking for a fight.

As soon as Ray saw them he was off his mark, running towards them though our number was down to 20 now. We charged, screaming: "come on you bastards." The Hibs mob were so surprised that they actually started backing off. I saw Ray and Mark wading into a section of their boys and we all followed suit – there was plenty to aim at. Mark, who had borrowed my brolly, was whacking into some skinheads when the police lifted him.After some mental battling, we regrouped at the start of London Road. Just as we started to walk up there, Hibs mob, organised at last, came round the corner. I saw about 200 of them running towards us. I had on a grey Lacoste jacket and I heard someone shout: "get him in the grey, get him, get him, kill him!" I tried to move against the wall at the side of the road but a punch caught me and then I was thumped against a car. The sheer weight was too much, and I fell down beside the wheel of the car. I felt all the boots coming in which nearly knocked me out, then I remember through the blurred vision seeing a copper and Jim, who held me up against the car and asked if I was alright. I think my head was booted against the car and the bang concussed me. I came to quite quickly, and started to walk again. The police arrested quite a few Hibs in that fight, and quite a few of us got a kicking.

We regrouped as best we could, about 17 or 18 of us, and made our way up London Road. We got our unity and strength back and with no coppers around, started running up the road. Hibs boys, thinking it was all over, were straggling behind their mob and we punched, butted and booted at every chance.

Just before Waverley we noticed a group of about thirty boys. We charged at them, they backed off at first. They kept their distance but slagged us for a few minutes. Then, when they had a few more boys (about 40 altogether), they came ahead. It turned into a running battle, with not much actual fighting.Traffic cones and bottles were the main weapons. After about five minutes the police finally arrived and sent us into the station.

We went into the railbar and you wouldn't believe the scene. Although most of us were cut, bruised and sore, we were hand-shaking and hugging each other. We did our city proud, we did it for Aberdeen. You would have thought we had just won an

Olympic gold for our country in a relay race.

Another memorable battle with Hibs was staged in 1985. The match was in Edinburgh again, and we had a good firm of about 400 with us. There had been no opposition all the way to London Road and by the time we turned into Easter Road I was quite far back in the mob. The leaders of the mob were about 50 yards in front, and not long after I was on Easter Road, the action started. Hibs Casuals, now totalling 250 or 300 at most had been waiting for us, and were now making their move. I saw a few bottles and traffic cones in the air and, as everyone else did, I tore down the road towards them. When I got down to the action there was a bit of a stalemate, a sort of no-man's-land where bottles, cones and the odd punches flew. Me and Glennie and Gory made a definite run right into the middle of their mob and started whacking everything. Aberdeen surged forward and that was it. I didn't see it, but one of the Hibs mob threw a bottle just before running, but was tripped up trying to escape. He was severely kicked on the ground and had to be taken to intensive care. He was in a critical condition – thank God he didn't die. Nobody, at least nobody I know, wants to kill…it's just a game. A few stitches, a few scars, fair enough, but death – that's a different story. I know that if someone was killed, most would stop immediately.

Just a few minutes on Easter Road, and a few side roads as well. I was well back with a few other lads, knackered and fed up of running. Suddenly a bar diagonally across the road emptied and about 20-odd big scarfers ran out at us. There were only about seven or eight of us at the time, but we went onto the road and met them. This was a really violent clash, heads were getting thumped, butted and booted. I never saw it coming, but as I was fighting off a couple of Hibs, another one swung a wire shopping basket into my face, and I felt my face tear. Ray ran in to the man and I backed off to the pavement, knowing my face was in a mess. There must have been a wire sticking out which tore my face – I got a deep gouge just below my left eye and a gouge out of the top of my nose.

The fight was calmed down by the police when they eventually arrived. I asked one of the policemen if I could get an ambulance, but the answer was: "no fuckin' chance, lad."

The fighting was over and we were escorted to the ground,
Inside, I went to the First Aid and had an antiseptic dressing
put on my face and nose. As I walked out of the dug-out area
underneath the stand, the Hibs support cheered my injury. I
simply smiled and waved. I wanted to get over that fence into
them, but I could wait. The doctor had suggested I go to hospital
for stitching, but I so terribly stupidly watched the match,
deciding to go to Casualty and Emergency in Aberdeen (I knew
everyone there and would feel more at home). I didn't half feel
like an idiot when they told me that the loose skin on my cheek
had died and they'd have to cut it off. I hadn't realised skin died
so quickly. It was a mess, and they couldn't even stitch it at all.
I believe the scar on my nose will almost disappear, but the scar
below my eye will be with me for as long as I live. Scarred for life
myself, and knowing that someone was nearly killed, you would
think I'd been affected. But no, next Saturday I was there, as
was everyone else.

We've had a lot of really good battles with Rangers at Ibrox.
One particularly enjoyable one was in 1984. We had won the
match as we normally do at Ibrox, and this helped to boost the
number of Rangers wanting to fight. There were about 350 of us
and we were really in the mood, after a few good fights at half
time, and a few before the match.

The usual stones started flying from far distances, and
immediately we made a move. That's one good thing about
Ibrox – there are big, wide spaces for battling outside the
ground behind both goals. We charged, and most of the Rangers
backed off. Some fought, but soon the stones got too much and
we had to back off. We moved on to the wide pathway along the
stand. Rangers filled the lane in front of us, and soon we were
swaying and charging into them, chanting "come on Rangers,
come on Rangers!" It's moments like these that make it all
worthwhile, everyone ecstatic with excitement. We chased
Rangers all the way through the lane, battering down anyone
we caught. Once out of the lane and into open space, the police
moved in with their horses. They managed to separate the
mobs, but not for long. Rangers charged, and we charged
through the police. The police line broke and masses of ASC ran
towards the Rangers.

ABERDEEN CASUALS
CITY OF ABERDEEN

To all you Dundee Scum,

We the Aberdeen Soccer Casuals think the letter that you gave
to us on Saturday the 6th April 1985 was, lets face it a heap
of bullshit. Calling us Bumpkins is not really appropriate
for the hardest bunch of lads in Scotland. Saying you told us
about Flares and Italian designers like "Armani".

Running riot in Aberdeen has never happened for any football club
especially the"Dundee Gays Club" which is about the best name you
are going to get. We don't mind so much you printing these leaflets
if the information in them were true, but all this shit about you
being no1 is not true and will never be .
Remember when you were still wearing scarves and all the time we
tried to tell you that we the Aberdeen No 1 Casuals had founded the
casual movement in Scotland . We gave a good display again at Rangers
and will continue to govern the Scottish Football scene and you will
experience our powers at Tynecastle when we waste you again.

Yours faithfully,

ABERDEEN SOCCER CASUALS NO1
HARDEST IN SCOTLAND.

Just before the clash, most of the Rangers originally charging had moved on, leaving only 20 or 30 Rangers to fight alone. Those that were left got trampled – I remember seeing Casuals falling over each other and piling up trying to get the boot in. We were quite close to the tube station now, and police were regaining control with their horses. Rangers re-grouped and what a mob. It looked like at least a thousand, and it looked like there was no way we could take them. We knew that if all the Rangers' fighters that were in Ibrox that day and all of us were put on an airfield and left to do battle, we would be wiped out. This was different, though, as you can only fight so may deep and wide in a city. We fought as a team, a garrison, watching out for each other and sticking close.

The police horses herded us away from that first tube station and off down the road towards the city centre. It's a long way to Queen Street from where we were fighting so we went into the first underground. I think most of the lads did, but I didn't realise that this tube station was on line from Ibrox. As I walked down the stairs a tube was just pulling up. The platform was solid Casuals and of course the train was solid with Rangers. The doors of the tube opened and Rangers had been sardine-crammed into them. The sight I saw then was unbelievable – at every door there were what resembled high speed windmills flying in at the tube, the lads were lashing into the train with their brollies.

Some sore-faced Rangers fans grabbed one of Aberdeen's lads' arms and held on, trying to pull him in the tube. Some boys hauled him out just before the doors closed, at the cost of an £85 Burberry jacket. Cheap at the price, for I wouldn't like to say if he would have made it to the next stop, had those Huns managed to drag him in.

The next tube was a carbon copy of the first, but the tube after that we got on and and back to Queen Street. We had a couple more fights around the station, but nothing special.

Over the years we have had quite a few good fights with Dundee. As I have mentioned before, the police are very well organised at soccer in Dundee or Aberdeen, so there is little action now at the match. However, if we stopped in Dundee on the way home from the south, or when there were semi-finals

FAIR CITY
FIRM

THE ABERDEEN SOCCER
CASUALS COME TO TOWN
ON NOVEMBER 5TH WITH
THE THOUGHT OF TAKING
OVER PERTH. JOIN THE
F.C.F. AND MAKE THEM
KNOWN AS THE ABERDEEN
SOCCER CASUALTIES.

and finals staged at a neutral ground, we got a good opportunity for a go.

I remember one time when about 25 of us got off a train, following some Dundee United men who had been slagging us, and got involved in a really mental fight. It was about even numbers for a start, and during the fight a Dundee guy started running away. I ran from an angle full into him, but came off second best. He had managed to swing a hook that caught me full force on the ear. My ear had a terrible, high-pitched whine after that but, though I was worried, I had to keep going on. On the grass beside the station, mannies were now running at us. They were steaming out of the bars now. I managed to deck a man with a suit on, but soon realised we'd have to go. We were being overpowered, and the mannies were now coming out with empty glasses. We beat a hasty retreat, we eventually just ran, a horrible thing to have to do, but it was that or glass-in-the-face job. This was a sad day, and one seldom spoken of. And it was especially sad for me, as my friends at Accident & Emergency told me I had burst an eardrum.

The longest chase I have ever seen was in Edinburgh. We were playing Dundee at Tynecastle in a semi-final. Dundee had held their own in some pretty heavy fights before the game, but after it ASC overpowered them. The road was full from both mobs squaring up. One Dundee man I recognised from fighting before the game was being really cocky and slagging us. Dave ran into the road from the pavement, jumped up, grabbed the guy's collar and cracked his head hard into the bearded guy's face. The lads cheered, and as we charged Dundee to a man got running. I don't know the total distance but the chase must have lasted for about a mile, right up Waverley Station. Their mob just got smaller as Dundee ran up the side roads all the time; Aberdeen's mob was getting smaller and smaller as everyone got knackered – only the really fit and the really keen kept up the pace. You hardly ever catch someone who's running because they've got so much more to lose.

CHAPTER 5

British Mobs

MOST ENGLISH Teams have their own section of troublemakers. They are of different sizes, have different names and wear different clothes; but they're all after the same thing.

Probably the most notorious support is West Ham's *Intercity Firm*, along with their close rivals, Millwall (*Boosh Whakers*). The largest mob is probably Manchester United's *Red Army*, who have a huge branch in London called the *Cockney Reds*. Chelsea have a huge hooligan element but, unlike most London clubs' thugs, they are not from any particular area (like *Arsenal Gooners* are from North London, Tottenham *Yids* are from South London, and Millwall are from the east). Chelsea Casuals are from all areas of London and the Home Counties, and so have different mobs with different names.

Leeds' *Service Crew* also have a very large violent group, who love to be in the headlines. Birmingham used to be a well organised mob of several hundred, but the police have come down extremely heavy on them. Seemingly, the Birmingham lads have stopped going to home matches altogether, although they still get a few hundred at away games.

You couldn't really fit English mobs in order of size but there are the really huge mobs, like West Ham and Chelsea, then lesser (but still large) groups like Middlesbrough and Derby County. Both of these mobs have stood up to the big boys on various occasions. Then there are the lower division teams' small but tightly knit mobs, like Blackpool and Darlington.

Although the really big mobs could have up to three thousand or more not everyone goes to every game. The smaller mobs could be as little as two hundred.

Some of these names may well have changed by the time you read this, but at the beginning of the 1986/87 season I asked around and came up with these names. This list is not supposed to represent a chart.

British Mobs List

WEST HAM — ICF (Inter City Firm) formed in the late 70's when they were skinheads

CHELSEA — APF (Anti Personnel Firm) half way liners were known as **Pringle Boys**

LEEDS — Service Crew A name generally given to all Leeds Casuals although actually is only the top 200

MANCHESTER UTD — The Red Army & Cockney Reds

ARSENAL — Gooners Quite a lot of blacks, Greeks, and Italians in their hooligan element

TOTTENHAM — The Yids or Tottenham Casuals

LIVERPOOL — Scouse Scallies

MANCHESTER CITY — Main Line Service Crew

NEWCASTLE UTD — NME (Newcastle Mainline Express) is the name for their young lads. The older men are called **Bender Crew** and travel by bus

LEICESTER CITY — Baby Squad Notorious for Stanley knives

BIRMINGHAM CITY — Zulu's Particularly impressive when they go to London

DERBY COUNTY — DLF (Derby Lunatic Fringe) Their ground is a favourite for violence with other crews

PORTSMOUTH — 657 Crew Hard Reputation

SHEFFIELD UTD — Blades another mob who started off as skinheads

PLYMOUTH ARGYLE — Name unknown but have a large hooligan following

BRISTOL CITY — Large crews

MIDDLESBROUGH — Middlesbrough were particularly evident in early 80's

BLACKPOOL — Bison's Riot Squad – Seaside Mafia Headline seeking with their "Let's smash up the stand"

fanatics

CARDIFF CITY	**Soul Boys** Much larger mob than the size of the club would suggest.
NOTTS FOREST	**The Red Dogs** is not well rated
LUTON TOWN	Their ground is well known for good battles even before Millwall rioted there.
ASTON VILLA	**Villa Youth** a bit quiet now

In Scotland, Aberdeen's Casuals are by far the oldest, biggest and best organised. Of course I am biased, but Aberdeen's superiority is a known fact. Aberdeen have well over 1000 Casuals, with a hard core of 200. Hibs and Rangers come joint second, with Hibs perhaps having the edge. They have around 400-500. Motherwell seem to have quite a lot of publicity, but they only have around 200 at most, and they only travel with 50. Dundee and Dundee Utd are hard to separate since they usually fight for each other – but I've seen them with a combined effort of around 400. Celtic, mainly because of the hassle they get from their own fans, have a few Casuals and little organisation, although seemingly they are growing. Hearts don't have much in the way of an organised mob, but so many of their normal fans fight anyway that they've hardly any. St Mirren have a really pathetic mob of about 100.

A couple of smaller clubs like Arbroath and Montrose have Casuals, and there are a few teams with no Casuals, but with support who are known to like a good fight.

I have drawn a list of Scottish clubs with Casuals roughly in order of their size. The list following is of the teams who have, small, unorganised groups who like a fight.

ABERDEEN	**Aberdeen Soccer Casuals**
HIBS	**Capitol City Service**
RANGERS	**Her Majesty's Service**
DUNDEE	**Utility Crew** or **Tayside Trendies**
DUNDEE UTD	**Utility Crew** or **Tayside Trendies**
MOTHERWELL	**Saturday Service**
CELTIC	**Celtic Casuals**

HEARTS	**Casual Soccer Firm**
ST MIRREN	**Love St Division** boosted by Rangers for the big ones such as Aberdeen
MONTROSE	**No Casuals** or **Portland Bill Seaside Squad**
ARBROATH	**Soccer Crew**
ST JOHNSTONE	**Fair City Firm**

CHAPTER 6

The Hundred Club

EARLY IN the season 1984/5 there was quite a lot of talk amongst the Casuals about starting a club. With the money we'd collect it was suggested that fines could be paid, match tickets could be bought and free buses could be laid on, and we could buy cards, stickers, posters and leaflets.

One Saturday when we had a home match, I decided to make the first move. I bought a pad and pen and made my way to the Schooner bar. Some of the boys had suggested that everyone should pay £5 a week so we could maybe have paid a trip to watch Aberdeen in Europe. I knew that it was simply not feasible to pay fines since some of the lads got fines for really stupid, trivial things, and they could amount to anything up to £500. So, I told everyone that the money was for free buses later on in the season, flip-flop membership cards, and a night-out function at the end of the season to celebrate winning the league again (we were that confident). Every club member had to be 18 or over.

The names and pounds came in thick and fast, and by the end of the day I had fifty-three paid members. The week after that the number went up to just over sixty. I didn't want just anyone to join either – I wanted people I'd see every week.

On the third Saturday I decided to spend some of the money straight away, as I told everyone of a laid-on bus to the Dundee United game the coming Wednesday. The bus cost £100 and was filled with members. I wanted to show them that the money wasn't going into my pocket. And I went to a printers and ordered 100 club cards, plastic-coated. I got them three weeks later, at a cost of £60. We were up to week ten by now, and I only gave the cards to fully paid members. The cards certainly made the members pay – everyone wanted theirs in their wallet. Some members were thrown out of the club for not paying regularly enough, and a couple paid £10 to join just for the card.

Well through the season, I started to go offshore again and so could only collect money at half the games. Still, the funds were growing. One match, missed through working on my rig, was a cup match in Edinburgh versus Dundee United. The trains were on strike and so there wasn't much of a support going down. A few cars full of Casuals went down and two buses were hired.

The minibuses were parked just up the hill from Waverley Station, and the lads went to the match. As they walked back after not much action with the Dundee United support, Hibs' Casuals made an appearance on Princes Street. The boys ran at them and tried to catch them, but in vain. One of the CCS (Capital City Service) shouted "We've got your minibuses."

They had. They must have had spies out who saw them being parked. One of them was smashed into a fence – the CCS had smashed the windows and let off the handbrake; the other had its wings booted in and three windows smashed.

Part of the deal with the van-hire company was that you pay the first £25 of any damage to the vehicles. Almost all in the two minibuses were members of the 100 club, and so it was agreed to pay out £50 for the two out of funds.

Nearing the end of the season, some members began to doubt if they would see anything for their money. More and more were suggesting that the last day of the season at Greenock versus Morton should be a party affair, paid from funds. This seemed like a good idea, as Morton didn't have any boys to fight and the season was over as a competition anyway, since we'd had a draw with Celtic at Pittodrie to win the league. No distractions, then, just a good-fun, boozy day out.

It was decided that this was the best idea. A bus was hired for £120 and we still had just over £200 for booze. In all, just over £350 was collected and spent.

The Day Out – Around 40 members turned up at the Art College, from where the bus would leave, and four non-members came, too. We took a fiver off them, which boosted the kitty by a score.

The bus was due at 8am, and minutes before then the Aberdeen FC luxury bus passed slowly by us. Everyone stood and clapped as they drove past. Some of the players waved and smiled, but a lot of them just stared. It has to be said that, although we idolised the players and the management, we had given them nothing but trouble since 1981, and most of them hated us.

Ev yone boarded the bus just after 8am and I paid the driver the £120. The bus was only hired to Glasgow to allow us to have a drink on the bus. Once out of Aberdeen I asked the driver if he would stop at Stonehaven for a carry-out.

Me: "This is a big day out for us but all we want to do is have a good laugh. We'll keep the bus in order, and if you stop when we want there's a good £20 in it for you on the way home."

"Sounds good to me, son, but keep the beers down while we go through the towns."

Everyone got off at Stonehaven and a large party of us made our way to the Spar store in the square. We knew that basically what we needed was lager – heaps of it. Nine cases of lager were marched out of the shop, followed by two cases of Pils and a case of Export. Ray and Terry were filling a cardboard box with crisps and biscuits, and Watty grabbed himself two huge double-handed jugs of cider. This lot came to around £170 so we went back to the booze rack to add some wine and champagne just for good measure. We got six bottles of white wine, two bottles of Pomagne and two bottles of champagne. When we got back on the bus, everyone was laughing at how much booze we had. It seemed impossible we could drink it all.

There was a three-hour drive from Aberdeen to Glasgow, and from Stonehaven to the depot in Glasgow, it was a solid party. The driver put the radio on and everyone started opening cans, drinking, talking and laughing. As the journey went on, the talking got much louder and the drink was being drunk faster. There was so much alcohol on the bus all you had to do was put your hand up into the luggage shelf and pull yourself was put your hand up into the luggage shelf and pull yourself a can. A couple of bottles of wine came on the go. No opener handy, but they were easily enough opened by shoving your thumb right into the bottle.

A few lads were handing round joints, and Watty was making a fast job of getting his body round the contents of that first cider jug. After about 40 minutes' drive I got the driver to stop, since all of us were choking for a piss. The whole bus emptied and three or four plastic bags of empties were taken out and thrown into the concrete bin in the lay-by. All the lads made one long peeing line which made me think of a sprinkler system being let off on a train. After a good shake we all went back onto the bus to fill our bladders again. It didn't take long – we had to stop roughly every half hour. The driver was getting pissed off, but he was getting well paid, too.

By the time we reached Perth everyone was boozy. The singing, slagging match was non-stop now and Brooner and Graeme were getting into a serious argument over who started the Aberdeen Casuals, who was trendy first – Bridge of Don or Seaton, who had Pringle or Lyle and Scott jumpers back in 1980. Everyone could see there were going to be blows, and so everyone did their bit to cool the two down. We managed eventually.

After two hours of solid drinking, everyone really was getting drunk. I took one of the nearly empty jugs of cider and started making a very crude punch. To the cider I added one bottle of white wine, one can of lager, one bottle of Pils and a half a bottle of champagne – a deadly mixture. It was christened *The Casual Potion* and all decided that everyone on the bus had to take a good drink of it. I handed it round and one after another everyone drank it 'till it was gone.

It was strongly rumoured that the cider in the jug to start with was not cider at all, but some desperate Casual's piss, but this time everyone was too drunk to care. Everyone was having a ball. This was the business: all mates together, we'd fought for each other often over the years. You knew many on the bus had saved your skin, and that you'd saved many of theirs. The feeling of unity and pride was strong, everyone knowing that anyone else on that bus would fight for them no matter what the

A/DEEN CASUALS

THIS HAS BEEN PRINTED FOR T E BENEFIT OF YOU
DUNDEE SHITS OF WHOM SOME THINK ARE NOW CASUALS

IT WAS ONLY A FEW MONTHS AGO THAT YOU WERE
STILL SKINHEADS IN FACT YOU STILL HAVE MORE SKINS
THAN YOU HAVE SO CALLED "CASUALS"

DO YOU REMEMBER THAT FOR THE LAST 2/3YEARS HOW
YOU USED TO TRY AND SLAG US AND SING "WHERES
YOUR SCARVES" WHILE ALL THE TIME WE WERE LAUGHING
AT YOUR SILLY "Y" CARDIGANS AND "STA_ PRESS" TROUSERS
ALONG WITH YOUR DENIM JACKETS AND ABOUT 10 SCARVES.

ITS SEEMS YOU HAVE DISCOVERED NAMES SUCH AS
"FILA, TACCINI AND ELLESSE" "WOW" WE WERE WEARING
THAT GEAR WHEN WE WENT STEALING THEM IN
HAMBURG ON OUR WAY TO GOTHENBURG YOU PROBABLY
THINK "LACOSTE" IS THE BEST THING SINCE YOU LAST
WON A CUP.

LETS FACE IT ABERDEEN WILL ALWAYS BE THE BEST
DRESSED AND WILL ALWAYS RUN YOU EVEN IF YOU HAVE
JOINED UP WITH THE UNITED SHITBAGS. WE RATE YOU
THAT LOW THAT A LOT OF OUR BOYS DONT EVEN BOTHER
COMING DOWN ANYMORE.

FUCK YOU DUNDEE SCUM, HEARTS HERE WE COME.

A/DEEN CASUALS HARDEST+TRENDIEST IN SCOTLAND.

odds.

All of us were so proud that we were the hardest in Scotland. We had proved it over the years, and it wasn't just us calling ourselves the hardest in Scotland – everyone knew it, from the police and the Casuals we were fighting to the punter in the street. We were the feared and notorious Aberdeen Soccer Casuals, and how we loved it.

Nearing Glasgow we realised that remarkably enough we had drunk most of the booze, and there certainly wasn't enough for a party on the way home. A kitty of £2-£3 was whipped up, and we gathered around £80. When we reached Glasgow we told the driver to park just up from Queen Street Rail Station, at the bus depot. This he did, and everyone waited while me and a half dozen of the lads went to reimburse the supplies of booze for the return journey. We purchased another four bottles of wine and five more cases of lager. These were put in the boot of the bus. There was still a fair bit of the original carry-out, so we just made the car park our bar, where we sang, drank and played the goat.

We told the driver we would all be back at 7pm, ready to leave. It was a nice, sunny day, so most of us left our jackets in the bus. Being drunk myself, I can't remember absolutely everything that happened on the journey from the bus depot to Glasgow's Station, however, I clearly remember a few things.

Just after we had started our walk we spotted a few trendies in the doorway of an arcade. One had a half-Celtic, half Everton ski hat on. They shouted abuse and when we moved forward they ran into the place. About 20 of us ran in – Magic! The place was full of them. They tried to fight us, but we kicked and punched them back against a wall. One bouncer tried to break things up, but someone grabbed him and smashed him in the head with his head. Even though every one of us was terribly drunk, natural instinct told us to get out quick before the old bill came. At least one machine was pushed to the ground, and a mob of around 20 Celtic Casuals were nursing bruises and cuts.

Everyone was itching now; the brains had completely gone. Anyone who looked trendy or game for a fight was challenged and, it being Glasgow, there were quite a few takers. Fights were breaking out all the way down the road. In the shopping precinct I heard a shout from the back of the boys. One of the lads, Veg, had been grabbed by two coppers and was screaming for help. What happened next I could hardly believe: about ten of the boys ran to Veg's aid. I saw a cap fly into the air, punches swinging, and then kicks flying into the coppers on the ground. I had seen violence against police in the grounds, hats being knocked off, punches thrown, mobs swaying into coppers with sly elbows and kicks put in, but this was something else. It didn't last long – reinforcements came running from both directions. There were some more struggles, but eventually four of the boys: Andy, Brooner, Veg and one other, were arrested. Dave was later found Not Guilty; the other got fines for Breach of the Peace.

Just after that, we met around forty other lads who had come down by train. One of them, Uchter, I was particularly happy to see, as he squared up a £50 debt with me. All the lads that went by train were so terribly disappointed that they'd missed the bill getting wasted.

We all moved off to Central Station. The railway station is a large part of any Casual's life. It is the focal point, the meeting place. Trainers were made for platform walking.

We boarded a train to Greenock, and arrived at Greenock station around 2.30pm. Knowing what a boring spectacle the game would be, with Aberdeen already decided champions and Morton already relegated, some of the lads just went to the bars in Greenock to listen to the jukebox, play pool, and have a couple more beers.

Me, Ged, Watty, Kyle and Sutly went away ourselves. We found a bar with a good jukebox and a couple of pool tables and had a laugh with some old Greenock mannies. After about half an hour in this bar we followed instructions and jumped a taxi to a livelier bar near the centre of town. There were more pool tables, and more young folk here so we stayed until it was time to go. A couple more of our lads came into the bar, and we all left about 4.20pm.

Just as we came up to the ground and we heard the full-time whistle go. When we joined the ones who went to the game, we realised that we hadn't missed much. There was a tiny crowd of around 3000, and a boring game. There had been a token gathering of Greenock youth on the terrace who challenged the lads, but with no segregation at Capilow, Jim and a few of the lads steamed into them, kicked their arses and chased them along the terrace. There was no more challenge from Morton.

We were escorted by police to the station, and when we were on the platform waiting for the train, everyone started to slag the coppers. I can't remember exactly what I said, but I really took two coppers down a few pegs and they were very upset. They told me to get out of the station, and that if I came back I'd be nicked. This wasn't a problem – I was immediately offered a lift in a car back to Glasgow. Some of the lads persuaded the old bill to let me on the train, and I was shouted back. I don't know why they let me back, it certainly seemed to me like a sign of weakness.

We arrived at Glasgow Central Station about 6pm and made our way towards Queen Street Station. We saw the train lads on their way and moved up to the bus depot. There was a bit of spare room on the bus now, with four arrests emptying seats, so those places were taken up by people who came to Glasgow by train. A couple of them were club members anyway, but had missed the bus that morning.

It was about 6.30pm when we arrived at the depot. We were quite surprised that the bus wasn't waiting for us, but we had agreed on 7pm. Some lads went for a pint in the nearest bar, and some bought fish and chips.

Just before 7pm a shout went up, and it was unmistakably a fighting shout. About a dozen of us were sitting on a wall near where our bus had been, but we all bounded off it and ran to the street from where the noise was coming. When we reached the street we saw scuffles on the road. Rangers ICF, just back from Edinburgh, were coming in numbers. We charged down at them. Surprisingly, they stood and fought for a while. The fun had only really started when the police came on the scene. Rangers dispersed and, dejectedly, we walked back up to the depot.

When our watches showed it was 7.15pm we really did start to worry. We phoned the company who had hired us on the bus. They said that they had no buses available and the man we had was a private contractor with just one bus. We couldn't contact him.

Time passed slowly, and tempers began to fray. A party was sent to see if there were any buses to Aberdeen that night. There weren't. We ran down to Queen Street to jump on the last train. The police stopped us and, though we explained our situation, they insisted on our paying our fare. Most refused to pay, but seven or eight paid the £16 single and jumped on.

We went back to the depot; still no bus. Everyone found it hard to believe what had happened: the bus was full of booze and everyone's jackets and jumpers. Some of the lads had money and hash in their jackets. Never had this happened before. One of us, Sutly, went away to Clydebank to stay with his cousin and get a train home on Sunday, but for those that were left (around 30) there was no such comfort. We were stuck.

I decided to phone the police. The last thing they'd want was a bunch of bastards like us roaming their streets on Saturday night, so maybe they'd lay on transport for us.

I laid it on the line, saying that we would be perfectly happy to stay and fight ("that is our hobby", I told them) but that there were Glasgow Casuals who knew we were here, and if they wanted to stop a riot they'd better get us out.

Within ten minutes we had a couple of top brass talking to us. They tried in vain to find out the story of the missing bus. Eventually they just suggested we take the strain and try to get on the paper train in Perth. Some bloody help – we always knew we could try that.

You can't get all the way to Aberdeen from Glasgow after 7.25pm, but there is a paper train that arrives in Aberdeen at 3am, but you have to sneak on or bribe the guard, and they aren't always willing. When you are arrested at away games the coppers will charge you and let you out of the cell just after your last train leaves.

You can always get a train to Perth. I have slept in the railway station at Perth twice: once in the toilet and once in a shelter, neither a very pleasant experience. Eventually we boarded a train to Perth at about 9pm. When the guard came across to us he just shook his head, laughed, and walked through to the next carriage. He couldn't be bothered with all the hassle, knowing full well that no-one had tickets.

BLOODY CASUALS

ABERDEEN SOCCER CASUALS
INCORPORATING TRENDIES
CITY OF ABERDEEN
SCOTLAND

T O   W H O M   I T   M A Y   C O N C E R N

As you may well know, Celtic are here on Saturday
TRYING to catch up on us in the violence league.

ADEEN
SOCCER
CASUALS

FUCK
OFF
TIMS

They shall never outsmart the ABERDEEN SOCCER
CASUALS, in DRESS or in BATTLE.

So on Saturday show them we are

T H E   H A R D E S T   M O B

I N   S C O T L A N D

JUST LIKE WE HAVE DONE TO MANY TEAMS THIS
SEASON:
Inc.......Celtic, Rangers, Dundee Utd, Dundee,
          Hearts, HIBS(on the pitch at Raith),
          MOTHERWELL and St Mirren.

Now it The Celts turn again, aren't they LUCKY.
Let's show them BASTARDS, that ABERDEEN have the
best team and the TRENDIEST, HARDEST "MOB"
in Scotland.

C O M E   O N   R E D S

L E T S   D O   T H E

B U S I N E S S

We had been moving no longer than ten minutes when a message came over the loudspeaker. Work was being carried out on the rails north of Larbert so we had to get off the train at Larbert, board buses, and be driven to Stirling to join another north-bound train. What a bummer – everyone was enjoying the fact that we had a seat for a while and our guard didn't care about the lack of tickets. We boarded a bus and luckily nobody asked for tickets either on the bus or on the train we boarded at Stirling. We relaxed a bit on the way to Perth.

We got to Perth just before 11pm and to our surprise and joy saw a freight train with a passenger carriage on it, bound for Dundee. We were so chuffed, there wasn't even a guard or anyone to check tickets, and Dundee didn't sound so bad as Perth. Dundee was much nearer home.

By the time we got to Dundee the drink had all but worn off, and everyone was a bit pissed off. It had been a long day and now all everyone wanted was to get home to their own beds.

There was a paper train due in around 2am, so we had over two hours to fill.

Steve suggested finding an Indian restaurant and doing a runner. I wasn't so sure about the runner bit, but I did fancy an Indian, and had plenty money for the bill. Me, Steve and John left the station in search of food. Approximately 300-400 yards into town we found an Indian sit-down restaurant. Steve was checking out the route we should run, and then we walked in. The place was quite empty, with just one couple and one table full of noisy, drunken Dundee United supporters. They had played Dundee that day and were celebrating winning a place in Europe.

An Indian came up with the menus and we ordered three pints of lager. The man serving us and the Indian behind the bar must have been about sixty each. Steve smiled "order as much as you want, boys, this is going to be a canter."

We ordered three mulligatawny soups, two chicken madras, one vindaloo, three pilau rice and three bindy bahji.

The mulligatawny soup was terrible – thin, burnt and oily – and that decided it. We were definitely not paying for this food. Meanwhile, one or two more couples were coming in. We overheard a couple next to us discussing doing a runner. I heard the guy saying "Look at him away through the back again."

We had a laugh to ourselves at how we were going to muck things up for them. After we'd done a shoot they'd put a man on the door to stop anyone else doing it. The couple probably wouldn't have enough to cover the bill. Still, it would serve them right, the poor bloody Indians were only trying to make a living.

The curry and the bahjis were a bit better than the soup, but still not up to standard, not like the Indians in Rose Street, Aberdeen. The waiter came up to our table when we finished and asked "Would you like anything else please?"

"Yes," said John, "could we have three Gaelic coffees please?" The waiter turned his back and walked to the bar. This was the moment. We gave each other the nod and stood up. Very briskly we walked to the door, to shocked looks from the couple next to us. When we got to the door we heard a grieving Indian's shout. We were off out the door and running like hell down the road. It was hard to run, choking back the laughter. We must have laughed solidly for 200 yards, then we walked the rest of the way back to the lads. There was no chance of those old Indians making chase. I only wish I knew what happened to the couple.

Back at the station, depression was setting in. Someone suggested taxis, so we asked a couple of drivers for a fixed price to Aberdeen. They said they'd do it for £40 which seemed quite reasonable for 70 miles – only a tenner each. Twelve decided to take taxis (including me), so a convoy of three left for Aberdeen. Our driver was a maniac, he was half drunk and half asleep. Three times he touched the kerb on the dual carriageway, both sides of it. The third time I said "You'd better keep your eyes on the road, pal, that's three times you've done that."

"Sorry son" he replied, "I'm just a bit tired."

"Then you shouldn't be driving for God's sake, do you want to stop?"

"No. no. I'll get some coffee in Aberdeen."

My nerves were badly frayed when we pulled in at my flat in Aberdeen. Nobody shared my agony – Steve, John and Ged slept all the way home and were none the wiser that they might have dreamed their life was hanging by a slender thread.

Terry and one other had started hitch-hiking when we left in a taxi, and got a lift with a long distance lorry. Two others successfully hitched it home, and about ten slept in the waiting room in the station until the first train to Aberdeen at 7am.

Over the next few days we found out what had happened to our bus. The driver left of his own accord because of the mess on the bus. I think he must have been used to doing pensioners' coach trips to Loch Ness or something, because the bus wasn't that bad. A bit of spilt beer and a lot of fag-ends and paper, but nothing really out of order. He left the jackets and booze in a shed at the large bus company that had passed the job to him. Of course he didn't make himself available.

All during the journey down we had been friendly to him, not in the slightest abusive, and we promised him £20 on the return journey. I suppose that's one of the things that makes this world such an interesting place – sometimes peoples' actions are impossible to fathom. Having said that, I hope the guy's next shite is a hedgehog.

ABERDEEN
CASUALS

1985
A/DEEN LOCOMOTION
NORTH EAST FIRM ABERDEEN F.C.

CHAPTER 7

Ambush

SATURDAY, AUGUST 17, 1985 on the way home from a match at Dundee we decided that something big had to happen at Motherwell the following week. God knows why we loved to fight Motherwell so much, but the feeling stretched back half a dozen years. Twice in 1983 we had demoralised their mob by entering their end of the ground and running them onto the pitch – the second time we had a booze-filled bus with exactly 40 nutters on it, who invaded their end when the game was going and made the whole terracing go berserk. The Motherwell support was chased on to the pitch, other Casuals on our end of the terrace started fighting police, and the game was held up for seven minutes. Motherwell have never run Aberdeen so I don't know why we hated them so much. Probably it was because they were the first team after us to be trendies, because they mouth off about us, and because some of their young boys carry Stanley knives.

We decided to have a meeting in the town some night during the week, and 8pm on Thursday night at 'Scaramouche' was agreed.

About 25 of the top boys were already there when I walked in just after eight. I bought myself a lager and sat with some boys. They'd already gone through the possibilities of taking trains to Portlethen or Stonehaven and boarding their train, or of everyone jumping out of cars and minibuses at the beach boulevard near the ground.

Almost unanimously it was decided that we should meet in Daisy's Bar (we knew it was on the police escort route) and pounce out of the bar as they crossed the road. The under-fives would take a lot of the police's attention – hopefully many originally escorting Motherwell Saturday Service would be trying to keep Aberdeen under-5s away from the visitors. We agreed to meet at 12 midday on Saturday. By 10pm that Thursday night half of the Casuals in Aberdeen knew the plan; by 10pm the next night everyone knew.

On Saturday me and Steve left my flat at about 10am. We walked around the town a bit and then went down to the station, where Bunter, Turdie and a few others were drinking pints outside the railbar. We spoke to them for a while and then moved on. Steve was to travel back to London on the Monday so he popped into the ticket office to find out the times of the trains. As we walked across to the bus station afterwards, I clearly remember saying: "You know I wouldn't be one bit surprised if there's CID watching the station from some of these buildings".

We walked up the town and quite a few people asked for confirmation that Daisy's was the place. One under-five boasted to me that his mob was going to bombard the police with missiles so they would get chased by them and leave the Motherwell SS to the mercy of the ASC.

Just after midday we walked into Daisy's lower bar. There were about twenty of the lads there, settling down to a pint and watching Football Focus. An Aberdeen Casual from Glasgow had phoned and told us what train they were getting. We had expected it to be the 11.05, arriving 2.15pm, and once the train had left we got the message that sixty Casuals were on it. After the phone call, the news was on the streets in minutes.

By 12.30pm there were about 45 in the lower bar and just before 1pm there were about sixty. At 1pm the upstairs bar opened, and we moved up to get the seats. On a Saturday there are film shows and go-go dancers, so we were kept amused. There were by now an almost constant flow of Casuals coming into the place. The management and the few regulars looked confused and amazed, and by 1.30pm there were well over 100 lads drinking and watching the go-gos. As time went on, it became clear that the number in the bar was exceeding all expectations, and more kept coming in. By 2pm the place was absolutely jammed – there must have been at least 160 in the place. All the top lads were there: some as old as 24 or 25; some married; some dads – all choking for a fight. We knew we could take anyone with this mob if we got the chance.

Just after 2.15pm someone ran in and told everyone that 70 of the SS had just got off the 11.05. The messenger had driven up straight away from the station to pass on the news. Everyone had itchy feet, we were dying to get out of the bar and into them. We all knew, though, that the best chance would be when they were right beside the bar.

Just after 2.20pm someone shouted the signal: "come on Aberdeen!". With what happened next you would have thought someone had thrown a hand-grenade into the bar. Tension was burning, everyone was swaying and jostling to get out first. As soon as I got out, I realised we had been a bit quick – the escorted SS were still on the footpath a couple of hundred yards away. I looked up towards the Beach Boulevard roundabout and saw about sixty under-fives tearing down the road. Aberdeen were everywhere, well over 200 of us, and everyone started chasing down the road towards the SS. Unlike the old days, I kept slightly back from the front runner. I had done my share of that and I knew that another charge would send me to jail.

As we ran back up the lane we'd just ran down, it split in two. The group I was in ran up the left-hand lane but police had blocked the other aide of that lane, so we turned round. The same story: We were trapped. There were about 50 of us and the chief inspector surveyed his catch. He shouted the instruction to lift every one of us. We had just expected to be escorted away from the Motherwell fans and to Pittodrie, but we soon realised that they really did intend to arrest everyone. Police from both openings to the lane were grabbing the nearest person to them, and every one of us was bustling himself away from the edge, into the middle of the pack. once we knew it was break out or be locked up, we started to sway one way, and the sway grew until everyone was pushing as hard as they could. The police gave way under the weight and those of us left scarpered down a bank and away. I ran along Commerce Street and up Marischal Street bridge stairs. I went into Freelands bar, where half a dozen other lads had taken refuge. I sat down out of breath, and one of the boys, Tommy said: "Hey min, did you see aabody getting lifted? Fuck that shit".

Our nerves calmed over a pint, and at about ten to three we left for the match. I had lost my close mates, Sutly, Steve and Stan, but I didn't think they had been lifted.

When we got to the ground we heard that there were so many people following the Motherwell mob that the police escorted them right back to the station and on to the first train home. Days later I read in the papers that a mob of Motherwell youths got off a train in Dundee for an hour and were involved in fighting in the city centre.

I went into the Beachend. Nobody knew how many arrests there had been, but it didn't seem like there could have been that many, because there seemed to be about 700 Casuals in the ground.

After the game I went back to my flat. There was still no sign of my mates, so my brother John phoned Lodge Walk police station and asked if any of the three had been lifted. "All three detained", was the answer. I could hardly believe it, especially not Stan, since he had never really been a Casual, and since, anyway, he was just recovering from a badly broken leg and had a walking stick with him at the time.

Because of the bad news, I didn't really feel like going out. I phoned my girlfriend, Jakki, and she came down to see me. We had a meal and a relaxing evening, it was getting late so I asked Jakki to stay.

At roughly 8am I became conscious after a deep sleep. My eyes focussed on two men, and suddenly widened – Jesus, it was two coppers. "Come on, Allan, it's time you joined your 47 mates, let's go". I protested: "couldn't you have knocked or something?". "No we couldn't, now get your arse out of that bed, you're going to jail son".

"What are you talking about? I haven't done anything wrong."

"That's not what all your mates have said. Now come on, let's have you."

"Do you mind leaving my room while I get dressed"

"Just get on with it."

I pulled the downie off me, I felt sick that the policemen were enjoying trying to degrade me in front of my poor girl. I felt quite confused and disgusted – surely I couldn't be lifted for something that happened yesterday? When I was dressed I turned to Jakki, told her not to worry and to phone my father and my solicitor. When the officer started to put on the handcuffs I saw Jakki crying in disbelief. My hands were cuffed far too tight, and were digging into my wrists. Then I was pushed out of my flat and marched out of the building. A couple of my neighbours, just coming back from the shop, watched me as I was manhandled to their waiting car. My God, this was degrading. They shoved me against the car painfully, and opened the back door. One of the policeman said. "I hear you're gonna have a go with the police this year are you, you bastards. Your Casual days are over, pal". With that I was bundled into the back, and all my weight went onto my wrists. The cuffs dug in painfully. One of the men said to the other: "Well, that was a lot easier than we expected, the door being open like that". I know damned fine the door wasn't open – they must have got a key from Stan's pocket.

Just as we were driving off, my brother came running out of my flat in shorts and bare feet. "What's happening?," he said, but the police just drove on, saying "you can see him in court". I looked back and saw him with his face in his hands.

When I got to Police Headquarters (Lodge walk) I went to the familiar charge box and was charged with Breach of the Peace. I was then taken to a small cell with no WC. At first I thought "great, no toilet" – that usually means you are just kept in for a few hours. About an hour later I was taken to an interview room and interrogated by the officer in charge. It soon became very clear to me that they knew almost everything. The coppers wanted the ringleaders badly, and were really putting pressure on the young boys to come up with the names of the main man or men. Many of them fell for the police threats and gave my name. About ten out of the 47 said I was the leader.

I gave a long statement and was then taken upstairs to cells. The policeman who took me upstairs actually started to biblebash me, I could hardly believe it. He looked in my eyes and said: "you know this, it doesn't matter what you lads do, whatever crime you commit and whatever punishment we give you, you will all answer to God, Jesus will punish you." I was amazed to hear this from a copper, and I said: "God may have a bearing on your life mate, but he has none on mine." "God has a bearing on every man. You will pay your debt to Jesus."

"You may hold the key just now, but I'm going to go a long way by myself. Hiding behind that God of yours, you'll never be more than a copper!"

His face was turning white now, and with a final "you will pay", he locked me in my cell.

The cells were badly overcrowded – three or four in each. I was put in a cell with Stan, another Casual and some guy who had been in since Friday night, Stan was glad to see me. He asked how long I had to visit, and I'd to tell him: "I'm here for the duration Stan, I'm nicked". I went to my door and had a shouting conversation with a few of the lads in other cells. Everyone wanted to know what it said in the papers.

Soon I was told that almost everyone had been asked questions about me. Some said they didn't know me, and a couple suffered for saying they had never heard of me. Once the talking stopped, I sat against the wall, and suddenly I really felt scared. If they wanted me that badly they might have me 'Remanded in Custody' and then if the case was on indictment I might get up to two years. My head was spinning and my stomach was tightening with frustration. The thought that I might actually not see Jakki, or anyone else for that matter, for two years was almost too much to bear.

More room was made for everyone, and by late afternoon me and Stan were in the cell by ourselves. We were delivered a plastic bag with chocolate, crisps, newspapers, puzzle books, etc. Whenever one of your mates gets lifted, it's the Sunday ritual to take in papers, smokes etc. Once you've been in for a weekend you know how important it is.

The food was absolutely disgusting. On Sunday night we had a squashed, warm pie with damp chips on top and watery gravy poured over them in a small plastic bowl. The pudding was beyond description.

Eventually, after many painful and worrying hours, I got to sleep.

On the Monday morning, the talking from cell to cell started again. Everyone knew that we would all have to go up in court that day and everyone was keen just to get on with it, At about 8.30am the solicitors started to pull Casuals out of their cells to find out the story.

Nothing but very grave news came back from the lads who had just seen their lawyers. Things were looking bad, and it seemed likely that we would be remanded in custody for at least a week. Seemingly the screws were fitting up beds for all of us over in Craiginches prison in Torry.

Around nine o'clock, Stan and me were called to see my solicitor, Mike Munro. Another three of the boys had him as their solicitor, too, and the five of us sat beside him and got a few things sorted out. He told us that our case was being treated very, very seriously, and that the Procurator Fiscal would try to remand us. Mike looked at me: "that's the quietest I've ever heard you anyway, Jay". What was there to say? – I knew the shit was going to hit the fan this time. I queried if it was legal for the police just to invite themselves into my property and arrest me in the manner they had, in front of Jakki. He simply said that as it did not directly affect my case there was no bearing on the manner of my arrest.

We went back to our cells pretty disheartened. Everyone was shouting now that we were all going to be remanded for a week. I shouted to them to stop being so pessimistic, as nobody really knew.

The usual Monday court went ahead, and plans were made for us all to appear in private after the weekend's other cases had been called. Hour after painful hour we waited, and another revolting dinner was passed in to us: some disgustingly fatty stew with smash. All of us just wanted to get in front of that PF and judge and see which way the cookie crumbled. We knew it was either minibus to Torry or walk across the road to the Atheneum bar.

Things were looking bad, but just after dinner Mike Munro looked into my cell and said: "everyone is getting bail". My heart jumped and I couldn't help shouting with joy. Jesus what a relief; what a weight off my mind. The news ripped through the cells and within seconds everyone was cheering, whistling and hanging on their doors with joy. The coppers had been constantly telling us that we would be remanded, and they were obviously sick. One copper walked up the aisle shouting: "shut up you bastards, you can still be charged with Breach of the Peace in here you know". A couple of loud "fuck off's" was the reply from the boys.

Soon after the good news they started to call us out one by one in order of age. At 21 I was one of the older boys. The oldest was a married 23-year-old, there were two 22-year-olds, and about half a dozen 21. Most were 19 or 20, although a few were as young as 16 or 17, and three were still at school.

We were handcuffed together in groups of five and then slowly led upstairs to the court. The reason we got bail is that the Procurator Fiscal knew he could not prepare the case within 110 days which is the maximum time you can keep anyone in remand before a trial.

The courtroom had been emptied of the public and the public seats were made into one very large dock. One by one we stood up and were granted bail. Even though I knew it was coming, it was still a relief when the judge himself approved bail.

Outside the courtroom we were set free from our handcuffs and all crammed into a witness room. In pairs, we were taken to collect our personal belongings. As people got their fags back, the room filled with smoke. There were no police in with us. Someone told me that they caught a glance of someone's statement, and saw the name 'Jay' a couple of times on it, as well as the boy's age – seventeen. I shushed everyone quiet and said: "which one of you grassed me up? There's a statement with my name on it, and it's a seventeen-year-old, so who's seventeen and looks guilty?". There was no reaction to this, just silence.

At last, oldest to youngest, we were being let out. We knew the press had been around in great numbers all day and half expected them to be waiting for us as we came out.

We were let out by a side door. The lane was packed with anxious parents and friends. As I walked up the lane I could feel the burning stares from the parents; I could almost hear them say: "It's those older bastards who've got our kids into this". But nobody drags anyone into being a football hooligan – everyone is there simply by choice.

My girlfriend Jakki, my brother John, and a few of the lads

were there to meet me. I gave Jakki a hug and a kiss and told her that I seriously thought I might not see her for two years. Apart from the really young boys who were whisked off by furious parents, most of the lads went into the 'Atheneum' to discuss our case without shouting.

BLOODY CASUALS

ABERDEEN SOCCER CASUALS LTD.,
INCCRPORATING TRENDIES,
CITY OF ABERDEEN,SCOTLAND.

To whom it may concern,

      Next year is 1985,therefore we will have to move with the times,to do this and to keep up with our English counterparts we will have to marr every Premier League football ground with appalling scenes of violence and mayhem,causing as much destruction as we can.

      I dont think that you realise the violent potential of our group and we will continue to live up to our name as we have so often shown in past experiences with Celtic,Rangers,Dundee Utd,Dundee and Motherwell fans,so therefore we shall continue to govern the Scottish football scene,we have the best team in the land and the mentalist bunch of boys.

      This is just a warning letter of things too come and if you dont take heed you will land up in your local Infirmary.So take this opportunity to respect us and to keep away and if you think you are able and willing to have a go,lets come ahead then and do the business

Yours Faithfully,

Y. D. M. T.

Y.D.M.T. the Branch of the
A/Deen Soccer Casuals.

CHAPTER 8

Porridge

Friday, January 17th 1986, Aberdeen Sheriff Court. Of 47 originally charged with Breach of the Peace for an ambush of visiting Motherwell Casuals: four had their sentence deferred for good behaviour; five were found not guilty; 30 were fined £100-£500 (£8000 in all): and eight were put on Social Inquiry Reports. Unfortunately, I was one of the eight. With so many getting fines when they expected Reports and even jail — I hadn't felt too bad — I thought that if the courts were being this lenient then maybe I'd a chance of just getting a big fine.

For six months this had been dogging my mind. It was six months since the ambush, and now I'd to wait another three weeks for reports. God I wished it could be over. I saw my social worker in Kincorth twice and she spoke to my father and my girl, also my work, who gave me a very good reference, The social worker's report was excellent. All eight had excellent reports: no-one recommended jail, most recommended a fine.

Friday February 14, 1986. The reports were too good. You just needed to look at the previous convictions each had to realise that none of the seven others were the angels their reports suggested. The eighth lad's report was not ready yet, and so he had to wait a further two weeks. The other seven were all jailed. I'll never forget these words from the judge: "Mr Allan. Six P.C.s since 1983. I'm sorry, 3 months imprisonment". I looked behind me to see a dismayed father and disbelieving mates. Three months is not a long time, but three months in prison – Jesus, that's forever.

We were led downstairs to the cells. It had finally happened. Somehow we managed to see the funny side of it, I suppose it just hadn't sunk in that we had been jailed. We were taken to the stairs one by one, and all our possessions were taken away to be listed. They take jewellery and watches – you won't see them again for a while. Those notes the copper put in a brown envelope I was going to spend buying the boys a few beers to celebrate the end of the waiting.

Once they had listed all our possessions we were put into another cell where some guys were waiting to go to court. Then it was out into the corridor where the seven of us were handcuffed to each other and led to a yellow van.

Out in the street, it was the last time we were going to see Union Street for a while, anyway. We were still trying to be cheerful and look on the bright side: it was only for three months. "Three months – Jesus Christ, two weeks on an oil rig seems like eternity."

Driving through the security gates, huge metal doors shut behind us. "Surely this couldn't be happening, no, not to me. I'm not jail material. What the hell are real convicts going to think of me?"

Three of us: me, Steve and Jambo, were to stay with the Cons until we got out, but the other four went through to Remand until the draft bus took them to Perth Detention Centre (since they were only 19 or 20 years old).

We were walked into the reception (I suppose you could call it that), and we got our handcuffs off. We were now out of the hands of the Grampian Police and in the hands of the HM Prison Officers, or screws for short.

Each of us were put into a tiny little box with a small, low shelf to sit on. I always thought that train toilets were the smallest rooms anywhere; now I realised I had been wrong. Our surnames were scribbled in chalk on the door – from now on it was second names only. As the screw shut the door on me my head sank into my hands: "Oh my God, what am I doing here? I was supposed to be going for a few beers now and offshore tomorrow. Now my solicitor is going to have to phone my company and tell them the score. My mother, my girlfriend ... how are they going to take it?". You just don't realise you're doing anything wrong, then suddenly you fall with a bang and "Holy Shit!" you curse yourself when you realise how many people you have let down, especially yourself.

I don't know exactly how long I was in my box but it must have been nearly two hours. Every news bulletin on the radio was the same story: Seven Soccer Casuals jailed for ambush. You'd think it was murder or something. There wasn't even anyone injured.

Eventually I heard my name and my door was opened. I filled in about four forms and was then told to strip and have a shower. They took away my clothes for storage and I could hardly believe the clothes they brought for me to wear. Small grey socks with a green stripe at the top; large worn red and white Y-fronts; grey, itchy-material flares and a blue and white striped shirt. The shoes were worn and flat, of thin black leather, and the pants and shirt had an 'Aberdeen Prison' transfer on them.

Then, dressed to a T, we were taken (me and Steve) through to A-Block (A-Block is for the Cons and B-Block for people remanded in custody waiting for trials). We were taken through an iron-bar gate and there it was, three stories of cells. "Jesus, it looks just like Slade Prison from Porridge".

We were handed to more screws in the A-Block glass house: "Here's the Casuals boys, watch them," said one screw who took us through. "Excuse me, is there any chance of sharing a cell with my mate", I asked hopefully. "Well I suppose we could manage that, son," was the answer. "Right, second flat cell 17, keep your noses clean and you'll be OK but we don't stand for any fuckin' around in here, you're not in fuckin' Pittodrie now boy". With radio being such a big part of prison life, the whole jail knew we were coming and we were kind of celebrities. There were quite a few Cons walking about A-Block getting tea etc. Quite a few were shouting, "Casuals, ya bastard" or "Oh no, it's the mental Casuals". This was really weird and a bit frightening – I just didn't know the score, didn't know what to expect. Maybe we'd be battered stupid, nobody to help us, nowhere to run.

"Hey Pat, how's it goin'?" I almost jumped with joy when I saw a guy I used to work offshore with. Pat: "Oh looky here, it's the Casuals, what the fuck are you doin' in here?"

Me: "Just got three months, I'm sick as fuck – thought I was going to get a £1000 fine."

Pat: "Three months! Fuck sake man, you're just in for a shit and a shave, I'm doing five years man, five fuckin' years."

When we got to our cell I suppose it *could* have been worse. It was very bare and a bit smelly but at least I was sharing with Steve. Our liberation day was written on our door card. April 14th doesn't seem that terribly long because although you are doing a three month sentence you automatically get a third off for remission. So, we were only actually in for 60 days, and today was one of them.

Of course we may lose remission – anything from three or four days for calling a screw a prick to 14 days for a fight, or maybe even more. Still, we had no intention of losing any days.

Pat came round to our cell with a bottle for water and asked us if we had a radio. We hadn't, and could hardly believe our luck when his mate went away and hustled us one. It was a tiny radio, attached with elastic bands to a PP9 battery, but to us it was magic.

Our door was shut and there we were. We looked at each other and tried to think of the best. The thing I was most worried about was waking up in the morning after being solidly asleep – I hoped my brain wouldn't freak out. At about six o'clock a screw came to the cell and we signed for our advance in wages. The two of us rarely smoke, but both bought a half-ounce of tobacco and matches for the £1.06 wage which some cons were actually paid for their week. Smoking gave us something to do, and anyway, if you've got spare tobacco (snout), you could buy juice, sweets, pictures posters, even hash. A half ounce deal of hash was hardly enough for a joint, but half ounce deals were easy to sell. Whenever someone got drugs of any sort in he would have to keep it very quiet or be hounded by tens of cons.

At roughly 9pm our door opened and we filled our plastic cups with tea. I hate tea with sugar in it, but I soon found there was no choice. Just after 10pm we heard heavy footsteps and the clink of light switches. So many times in the next 60 days I was at a really important part of a book and 'Clink', the light goes out.

That is one of the most infuriating things – nearly as infuriating as the light clinking on at 6am.

At least when you're asleep it doesn't matter that you're in jail. That first night when the light went out I looked up to the arch ceiling and nearly cried with frustration. I could hear some man screaming curses to nowhere and others screaming "Shut up, you noisy bastard". I though if I slept hard enough maybe I'd wake up and find it had all been a dream.

6am; clink of the light going on and the door banging open – they give you an extra hour's sleep at weekends. I wasn't dreaming I really was here, and not in control of my life any more.

There are no WCs in the cells, or "peters" as everyone calls them, just plastic piss pots with lids, and first thing every morning is a big procession of bleary-eyed cons, piss pot in hand, heading for the toilets ("arches") to slosh them out. The prison term for this is "Slop-Out". In the sinks there are rows of men washing and shaving. Some wheezily cough, hack, and spit repeatedly into the sinks. So revolting, I always waited till the last minute before washing so that the sinks were quieter.

When we got down to the dinner hall I was totally over-whelmed at the number of cons, many I recognised just from drinking in various bars and some I recognised just from seeing them begging in the street or drinking with down-and-outs. Three men in turn came up and asked how long we were in for and told us that a screw would give us a seat when all the rest of the cons were seated. Everyone sits in tables of four and some cons will sit on the same seat for years. As cons are liberated, newly-jailed people will take their seats. sometimes a con can wait for weeks or months before getting a seat with his mates. We were lucky and sat together on our fourth day there.

One thing that was a very great relief to me was that nobody seemed to be hostile, in fact they were quite the opposite. One guy, Tony, who used to drink with a couple of Casuals I knew, gave us pillows and jumpers; another con gave us magazines. It was really quite overwhelming how well we were being treated by some cons. I think the main reason is that they were glad to see some respectable, clean youths instead of more alcoholics and tramps.

Quite a few cons came up and asked us about Casuals they knew and even some screws spoke to us about football. I suppose the screws were the most surprising thing of all. I had expected them to be like coppers, but no. Some of them could be a bit cocky but on the whole they were quite civil – more civil by far than American toolpushers on oil rigs.

I compared jail to the rigs quits often. Similarities were: no football, discos or beers, and mainly no women. (I think pornography on every Peter wall just made things worse). The main difference was that the food was another world on a rig: and you only did 14 days, not 60. More important, you got about £600 cash for your fortnight; and a grant of £27.50 on release from jail. I always wondered why they give you money when you get out of jail, but now it is very clear. So many people in jail are thieves and housebreakers, and if you let them out of jail with no money they're going to do a job straight away. At least if they have a grant it gives them money to last them until they can get unemployment benefit, and maybe give them a chance to go for a better life.

Of course, not everyone in jail is a bad criminal. Some are in for driving offences, some are in for fighting, and some for smoking hash or selling it. Some are friendly, seem sensible and intelligent – often more so than screws. I often wonder what they are in for but sometimes it's not cool to ask. After saying that, there are also a large amount of depressing cases: men accepting the fact that jail is part of their lives. Crime and Time, and many seem not happy, but contented.

Scars and tattoos are in abundance. Boredom leads cons to tattoo each other and some mens' hands and bodies are in a terrible state. Most are ugly, but some are quite humorous – like one guy I saw in the shower had a big 'W' tattooed on each cheek of his arse. Once we got our first weekend over it was on to the work sheds. Some cons did nothing and got paid £1.06 a week; and some wove the nets for £1.90/week plus 15p extra for every net completed. Experts managed three nets per week, giving them the huge wage of £2.35. Me and Steve decided to give the weaving a go – to hell with making less than two quid a week. We picked up surprisingly quickly. It did seem ironic that we were paying our debt to society for our little war games by making camouflaged nets for Maggie's big war games. Still, we kept on weaving.

When we left the sheds we were given a pat-down search and went through to the dinner hall. We got our first letter from one of the boys. It's magic getting a bit of sympathy and a laugh, especially from Terry, as he had eaten a few plates of porridge himself over the years. I knew that this would be the first and last sentence for me. Not that I have anything against porridge (it's quite nice well salted with milk) it's all the other shit you've to go through.

I also got a letter from my girlfriend, Jakki. It was not so nice as the ink was smeared in places, suggesting fallen tears. Sometimes letters make things worse, reminding you – not that you need reminding – of where you are. I always thought that I was too smart to get jailed.

In the afternoon I was taken to a finger-printing room and had three copies of my prints taken. They don't let you forget you're a criminal. Most people in Britain are criminals in some way, or have been: trespassing offences, driving offences, littering offences, a little tax evasion. The name *criminal* just means you have broken the law, committed a crime, but you are only called a *criminal* if you've been to jail for it.

I do not see myself as a criminal – just as a person who was involved in something which seemed just good fun at the time, but unfortunately, sometimes affected people not directly involved. But I am not bitter about being sent to jail. I don't really regret those years as I had a lot of fun, but I do realise that it was wrong, and jail in my case was just.

The days of the first week passed slowly but surely, and my spirits weren't too low. Jail was not nearly as bad as I had anticipated – people really were being helpful. Also, with the football hooligan thing being of so much public interest, cons and screws alike would ask questions trying to find out what it was all about. Most cons found it amazing that we got jailed for something that could not make us money if we got away with it.

117

When I was about 10 years old I was caught stealing sweets. The embarrassment is still very clear in my mind, and since then I haven't stolen so much as a packet of Polos. For many around me in jail, though, it was their living and some accepted that part of the lifestyle included the odd sentence for the times they were caught. In the sheds I could hear cons discussing ways of "doing a chemist" or "doing a hotel or bar", and some discussed "doing a country post office with a shooter". The last was spoken of little although one or two cons were inside for armed robberies, I have heard about jobs you could do: "water-tight, can't fail", they'd say, trying to impress. I would listen and nod all the time, thinking "if it's so water-tight why didn't you do it," and "why are you in here then if there's so many easy jobs to do".

By Friday I was quite settled and trying to think of all the good points. At least I'll definitely not go back to football after this. Maybe the shock will really stand me on my feet and motivate me to make something of my life. I told myself then: "this sentence is good for me," and I definitely believe today that it was.

On my second Sunday I got a shock. Tony came up to our peter and told me there was a story I'd be interested in in the newspaper. I looked at the open paper in Tony's peter. My heart raced ... half of a bloody page was all about me. A screw came to the door and said: "Aye, you're in the big time now sonny, you'll never be able to go to another match in your life".

I'd had police investigators at my flat asking questions about the 100 Club. What they wanted to know was whether or not fines had been paid out of funds as was rumoured. When I told them no fines were paid it was left at that. When the reporter heard that no fines were paid he told me they would not do a story on it. He asked me for a shot of an old collection book just to show his boss that he had done his homework. Promised to send it straight back to me. I didn't really want it anyway, but that was the last I saw of it.

I had heard so many times of people taking papers to court for lying and exaggerating, but it took this story about me to finally open my eyes about these papers. I only wish people could realise what these papers are doing and stop buying them without having an experience like I had. Reading that report I felt so cheated, and I have never bought a gutter press paper again.

Millions in Britain still buy these papers. I don't need to name them all because for some funny reason they are all half the size of real newspapers. There are enough fact newspapers in every part of Britain and I hope eventually the people will open their eyes and stop buying this daily soft porn with spatterings of fact.

My solicitor came to see me about it on Monday, found out what I really had said and sent off a letter of complaint. Unfortunately we couldn't really sue, for it's more the way they phrase things: suggesting rather than stating. Slowly I managed to push it aside and the bitterness left.

Visits came every two weeks and often threw me into depression. Apart from my admission visit the first of my four allowed visits was on my second Tuesday in, day 12. My father, mother and girlfriend came to see me and I was nervous as hell.

The visit went OK – I think my folks were relieved to see that I didn't look like a nervous wreck. I know that they thought my encouraging letters were just to stop them worrying. After ten minutes my parents left me with Jakki. There was no glass between us, just wooden cubicles with an open top and little bench seats. Two screws watched at all times. I reassured her that things were OK. God she looked beautiful. How I longed to hold her, just to hug and kiss her and tell her to get me to hell out of here. It was not to be. I got a peck on the lips at the end of the visit. Over for another two weeks. Thank God.

On the second Wednesday, day 13, we got our first letter from Sutly (one of the lads in Friarton, and a good mate). Things weren't too easy down there, much stricter. With marching, circuit training and locked up hours every day. They had to make bed blocks like in the army, and when locked up they had to sit on their chair and not on their bed. If caught sitting on their bed they would he put on Governor's report. The Governor would decide what punishment was right. They also had to run a mile in a certain time or they would lose two days. Sutly said he was made to run five times round the football pitch before starting his mile. The most infuriating thing for them in

Friarton, however, was that every book had its last page ripped out. What a sick thing to do.

On the second Thursday, day 14, we were taken off the sheds and put to work on the pass. In A-Block this job is: cleaning the toilets, handing round the tea at night, and taking in everyone's plates and cups after each meal. This was a much better job. Tony, who was the head passman, arranged it with the screws. The best thing about it, the pass. was that, unlike before when we were locked up ('Dubbed up') after work for the night, we got recreation from 7pm – 9pm. What a boost that was – table tennis, pool, darts, TV and daily papers. This made things a lot more acceptable.

On Friday I was told that I was picked for Saturday's game. Every Saturday there is a game of soccer, half an hour each way in the exercise yard. With me now working on the Pass I was eligible for a game. Craiginches make the nets for Aberdeen Football Club and in return they get old training kits. I was quite chuffed to be playing in an old pair of Alex McLeish's horts.

The game was Aberdeen v Glasgow and turned out be a ridiculously dirty game. I was warned that the games were tough, but really this game could more or less have been played without a ball. At one stage I had the ball and was turning against the wall when a Glasgow con plastered me against the wall and took the ball. I started to watch my legs and gave as good as I got. Unfortunately, what I got kept my legs in pain for a week, and I still get a twinge in my knee every so often from that match.

There are two balls each Saturday. If you kick the ball over the wall it's a goal to the opposition, and if you kick the second ball over you lose the game. I felt rather hard done by in a different game when someone booted the ball over the wall with a painful, smashing deflection off the side of my face. They got a goal; I got a ringing face.

The final result of this game was: Aberdeen 12 – Glasgow 7. Still, Aberdeen had a lot more to choose from.

Me and Steve did 150 press-ups a day. We were not allowed to go to keep fit as our sentence was less than six months. The class lasts for half an hour and is only on a Friday evening.

The food was one of the worst things about being inside. I remember one day we were given: green curry, smash, watery cabbage and skirly all on one plate – a sickening combination. At lunch time, which was the only proper meal of the day, me and Steve had a routine – he gave me his smash to thicken my soup and I gave him my semolina and rice pudding and milk puddings which we had most days. The stews etc. were very fatty, with almost no meat, and the fish were tiny and unfresh. I remember one day the soup had a very weird taste. Cons work in the kitchens so I asked one what it was. He said that they put a load of custard in the pot and stirred in a tin of mixed spices to disguise the taste.

On Saturday night we got a real treat in the form of a fresh apple. This would be saved and eaten slowly later on at night.

At weekends from 5-10pm lights-out, your door is locked. What a terribly long time that is. You have to try to not sleep for if you do you may not sleep at night.

During weekdays, exercise is immediately after lunch. For an hour you walk round and round the exercise yard, all the time the ground getting more and more covered in vile spits. It's quite nice, however, stretching your legs. As soon as there is any hint of rain everyone is taken straight away for inside exercise. The reason for this is that no con has water-proofs or a change of clothes. After a few weeks I wanted so much just to feel rain and wind in my face.

After I started the third week my spirits were quite high. I was managing well not to let myself sink into depression. Working on the pass with some cons with a good sense of humour helped me through each day.

One very unfavourable job for passmen (even worse than counting the old socks and pants) was collecting the shite-bombs. With no WCs in the cells, some cons, in desperation, would lay down a newspaper or a bit of blanket, crap in it, fold it up and throw it out of their window. Luckily I did not do this job but I heard passmen who, wheelbarrow in hand, picked up many of the bombs. You can never know which window they came from either, as they would throw them to left or right of their own window.

Neither Steve nor myself had to stoop this low, although a

couple of times I had to run for the arches at slop-out or exercise when our doors were opened. Our friend Sutley in the Detention Centre said that the cabbage patch was directly below rows of cell windows. The chef was baffled as to why none of the little bastards would take the nice fresh boiled cabbage with their meals.

Craiginches is basically a short-sentence prison (sentences of up to 18 months) although any length of sentence can be done by over 35's. Many young men, however, can wait for months before there is a space in a long term prison like Perth, Edinburgh or Peterhead. Because it is for short sentences there is little homosexuality which pleased me, as the thought of it makes me cringe. There were stories, though, of cons being stuck up another in the shower. No doubt some of them are true. One Glaswegian who had 12 years of a recommended 15 still to do spoke to me in exercise one day. He had not felt a woman in just over three years and he knew he wouldn't again for at least 12 years for they would only let him out then if he had behaved. He told me he hates with all his might the cons who involve themselves in sex amongst each other, as it is "giving up to the bastards", letting them win and taking away any self respect a man has left.

I certainly don't admire the crimes for which these long-termers serve. But I do admire the way some of them keep their dignity and sanity. Many keep themselves and their peter very clean and tidy, polish their floor and iron their shirt at the weekend.

The support in the form of letters from friends and relatives was fantastic. I only wished I could write more replies – it was difficult as you were only given one letter a week. If you wanted more you had to buy them out of your wages from the canteen on Fridays. Out of our weekly £2.30 I bought two letters every week. I enjoyed writing very much. Me and Steve for interest's sake shared all letters. A lot of letters were sent to us both from the lads but we shared girlfriends and family ones as well. Every endeavour was made to keep boredom at bay. Letters flowed in fast and furious – one day three, next day five, next day seven, then two. All in all, from 27 people we received a staggering 145 letters and cards in 60 days.

This is a note to congratulate all you ABERDEEN SOCCER CASUALS, on yet another successful season at the top of the League.

We are as superior on the Terrace and Streets as our team is on the field, but although the team can finish the season today we cannot claim our trophy until next Saturday when we play Hearts. They must have spent alot of time making inteligent suggestions to come up with a completely origional name, Heartz Service Crew, the only team we have yet to take away from home.

Anyone who misses this one can't call themselves an ABERDEEN CASUAL, miss this one and you might as well wear your scarf next season.

So its Celtic today and I wonder what those stinking tramps are going to call themselves, probably take a name from England like Rangers chocolates, Jesus Celtichow can you be so far behind the times, even St Mirren were converted before you. Ha Ha makes me laugh to remember us chasing them all the way from that bridge to the station and through their market.

When your out celibrating tonight, anyone who looks suspicious or smells fucking awful, pull him up and if he says "By the Way", batter fuck out of him.

There was excitement on Saturday in the form of a football coupon: 15 fixtures and you had to forecast them all. On average, around 20 paid the stake of a Mars bar, and if you were the only winner you were a rich man. We were in our peter when the full time results were read out, and when I wrote all the scores down things were looking pretty good. I had eight right and only one other had eight. There was only one late kick-off result to come in. It was an English Third Division match – I can't remember the sides, but I had a home win forecasted and the other on eight had an away. It was all on this game.

When the late results were announced just after 5pm, home win it was. Me and Steve burst into a massive cheer and did a dance on our bunks. "Magic, fuckin' magic! We did it!"

On the Sunday I was handed my prize – only 17 this week, but I was happy. We had a whole bar each on that Sunday and at least half a bar every day for the next week. Apart from receiving letters, the Mars was the highlight of the day.

The following Saturday there were 20 Mars in the coupon, and four people got eight games right. Steve and me were two of them and so collected ten Mars bars to restock the diminishing supplies.

Gambling was rife: from coupons to individual matches, to table-tennis and darts. Anything from one roll-up (snout) to a half ounce of tobacco would be stakes. For the Grand National 40 cons, including me, put in one Mars and we drew a horse number. My horse, Plundering, came nowhere, but West Tip was so fancied that the guy who drew her was offered five Mars' for his horse; another offered him half an ounce. He kept onto his horse and won 40 Mars.

Another competition was backgammon. Only ten could play, and we played best out of three knockouts. I won the first competition without losing a game and claimed my prize, nine bars, but was out in the first round the next week by some hot shot who was just jailed for his part in drugs dealings.

I lost a Mars when Aberdeen went out of the European Cup to Gothenburg but Steve won one for Arsenal beating West Ham. On the whole our gambling was a big success.

With both of us just buying a half ounce of tobacco a week and gambling going as well as it was, we could afford a little luxury at canteen. Friday was canteen day – what an excitement. For most cons it was a relief, at last they could buy smokes again. Most of them are on to douts (fag-ends) by Tuesday or Wednesday. We always had some tobacco left and large fag-ends although we never smoked them. We saved them up and gave them to cons who had helped us when we first came in.

As we were partners in everything, me and Steve bought mutual supplies, We had £4.60 between us, and we spent it carefully, One ounce tobacco, £1.90; two packets cigarette papers ('skins') 10p; two boxes matches, 12p; three canteen letters, 16p; one bottle apple or orange squash, 60p; three packets of biscuits £1.06; one Kit Kat to share, 16p. This came to £4.44 – magic!, enough for eight McCowans toffees (four each) and making the total cost £4.60. Packing our goodies away into our peter was a great feeling. We diluted our fruit juice into an empty squash bottle and rested them against the bars outside the window – this worked as an excellent fridge. We had to admit that we managed well to keep our home as liveable as possible.

Sometimes if a con feels he is in danger from other cons he can ask to be put on protection, which simply means that you stay behind your door, only getting out to slop out in the toilets. At meal times food is put into them on trays. There were three men on protection in A-Block when I was there. Sex offenders are hated badly in jail. They are known as *beasts*, and these three men were beasts. The beasts are a target for other prisoners. One reason for this is that they should not be in the same building, under the same type of punishment as sick men who commit vile acts on small children, young girls, and women.

Although I have never seen it, I have heard that in a particularly sick case the screw will sometimes leave a beast's door open for the cons to go in and batter the shit out of him. They don't tell anyone to do it, just leave the door open. If a man commits a sex offence against a young child I feel he is not sane and should be given medical help and therapy. Keep him off the streets of course, but don't just bung him in jail for a couple of years. That probably won't help the man.

On Sunday nights there is a request show on the local radio

station, Northsound, between 10 and 11pm. It is almost all requests for us jailbirds and my God, what a shot in the arm you get when you hear your name over the airwaves, and hear one of your songs. We listened every Sunday and every Sunday we weren't disappointed. Some Sundays just one dedication – on one occasion we got three. You really find out who your mates are if you do time. 'Out of sight, out of mind' was apparently the case for some people who I had considered to be close friends. However, on the whole, contact from outside was fantastic.

Saturday, March 13 was a brilliant day, for it was the half-way mark in our sentence. I felt so, so happy and relieved: we had reached the peak and now it was all downhill. It seemed like I had been in jail for around three months but I was not too depressed. I knew at least that I was finally winning.

Every Tuesday a screw would go out to a shop and buy things like batteries, lighter fuels etc. Cons would fill in a PPC form (Personal Purchase Certificate) and the price would be deducted from the money you came in with. I bought a lighter, lighter fuel, and a battery for our radio. The lighter fuel was kept by the screws and could be filled up every morning. I soon found out that there was a market for PP9 batteries. You could sell them for half an ounce of snout. I got to it straight away, finding old batteries and swapping them for new at £1.49 a go. You were only supposed to have one battery at a time, but if I was questioned as to why I purchased so many I simply said: "it must have dropped", or "must be faulty or something", I bought one a week for four weeks. When I sold them for half ounces this meant I didn't have to buy snout at canteen on Friday and so I could spend the entire £2.30 on letters, drinks and sweets. My God, I was rich.

The next two weeks passed reasonably well, but although I managed to shrug it off quite well I did have very low moments. I often thought about going into the shop I knew was directly across the road from the main gate, I dreamt so many times of entering it and buying a bottle of Lucozade and then walking down to the river Dee drinking it. How I longed just to walk to a shop in the rain, spend some money and walk home. How I longed for a cuddle with my girlfriend, to sleep in in the morning – even just to wear my jeans. Two months doesn't seem very long, but in confinement it certainly is.

Thank God I shared with Steve and not some grotty, stinking manny. We shared the work, the food, the letters, and we shared our feelings. Recreation in the evenings was not compulsory and sometimes one of us would leave the other behind his door for a wank to the women on the wall while the other went to read papers or watch TV. Well you can't expect us to go 60 days without an empty, can you?

As time went on, days seemed longer. When I had only three weeks to go it was hard not to think about getting out. Come on, come on, only three weeks – magic – when we wake up it'll be only 20 days. Nerves were getting stretched. I was beginning to freak Steve out about how long we had to go. How could I help it? – we had only 19 days to go now: three more weekends, just two more Tuesdays. There were so many different ways of looking at it, and I thought of them all constantly.

On the third Saturday before I got out, Aberdeen had played Dundee at home, and there were reports of trouble and arrests. I soon learned that Terry and Ray had been lifted. Somehow Terry managed to get his 'Breach of the Peace' charge dropped straight away, but Ray was charged and remanded in custody. That meant he would have to come through here in B-Block until his trial came up.

Cons cannot speak to people in Remand for various reasons, one being that some of the cons may be involved in their case. but they are out for exercise in the morning when we are cleaning the toilets etc. I had been promoted to Showers Man (what a title, eh?), and had to put my wooden shower boards out to dry every day. I made sure to ask a screw to let me put them out slowly, and have a quick shouting conversation with him, just long enough not to piss the screw off so much that he might put me on Report.

That was a hard way to chat. The only time you get a good chance is at church. The church is segregated, but if you both sit in the middle you can talk for a minute before and after the service. The Sunday I had seen Ray was Easter Sunday, and the pews were all full. The reason for this devout show was that a Cadbury's Creme Egg was given out every Easter to all who went to church. Some of those poor bastards could remember that from last year. The only other time when religion appeals to the masses is at Christmas, because then you get a cracker with smarties and two cigarettes in it. And, apart from the chat with Ray, the service got us out of counting the socks, pants and towels – a particularly revolting job.

Days dragged by amazingly slowly, but I clearly remember day 47, April Fools day. "It's actually April, Steve, we are out on the 14th of this month, brother". Steve's face lit up when he realised it was this month now. It was a Tuesday, and Tuesday means film night – the one night of the week that we get a video. On this Tuesday some science fiction film was on. I don't really like science fiction, but I got totally lost in this film, thoroughly enjoying it. When it finished I was still in space, and when the lights went on I was hit in the face with the vile reality of where I was. As I walked in the line of cons being directed and supervised by screws, I was once again thrown into depression: "Why, oh why am I here? What I am doing in this fucking place?, please somebody open those bloody gates and let me free." On Wednesday, April 2 the depression was gone – it was just too close to let myself be depressed and weak. Amazingly, Thursday, Friday and Saturday passed remarkably quickly and on Sunday 6th we felt fantastic. Some con had been hiding some home-made hooch in one of the toilets that Steve had been in charge of cleaning. Yeast, sugar, water and smashed apple were the ingredients and we had to admit it did smell like booze. It had a kind of two-day-old-Kestrel aroma about it. We had a whole plastic bottle of it, and the party was tonight.

As soon as our door was dubbed it was out with the hooch and out with the plastic cups. With a big smile, Steve takes a sniff from the neck, holds it up to the light: "Hey brother, lets you an' me fill our tubes with some of this shit-kicken' licker. I'm gonna tell them fascists to stick their motherfuckin' sweet tea up their ass!". With that we were off. I don't know if we really got drunk, maybe a lot of it was psychological, but one thing for sure – we had a ball and danced to almost all the records on the top 40 show, and many after.

For the remaining seven days I suffered what they call Gate Fever. Everyone knew the Casuals were out soon and everyone kept mentioning it. The last weekend was the worst as you are dubbed up most of the day, Saturday eventually passed, and when the door closed just before 5pm on Sunday we knew the big wait was on. We could hardly speak with excitement. Already photos and letters were packed, and anything that was asked for was distributed amongst people we liked. Our radio would be handed to Pat, the guy who got a shot of one for us two months ago. He will sell it for an ounce of tobacco, or hire it out for a quarter oz a week.

We made lights-out eventually and the request show was good and loud. All the usual prisoners were getting their requests, loved ones saying how much they loved and miss them. Then I heard the DJ say: "Here's one for my boyfriend Jay Allan, it's his big day tomorrow. Tell him I love him and I'll be there at 6am tomorrow morning". The record was *You're The best Thing* by the Style Council. My stomach tightened, my heart was pounding, and I felt my whole body would explode with emotion. I must have made it to sleep around 1.30am.

Just before 6am I heard familiar footsteps and the chink of light switches. I bolted upright: "Steve, Steve, it's there son, we've done it, we've fuckin' done it!" Steve threw off his blankets, threw me five and, face bright red, gave me the most vigorous handshake I have ever had.

We said adios to the lads and with our doorcards walked through to reception. We were put into those tiny boxes again and told to strip. Once stripped, a screw handed me a coat hanger covered in my own gear. Those socks felt so soft, my Y's fitted, oh my God! – what a feeling stepping back into my jeans. how I had waited for this. Fully dressed I went up to the desk, signed for my earrings, gold chain, watch and money, then we were taken through to the last door. We signed one more document, and the screw said: "You're now a free man".

With adrenalin flowing out of our ears, we walked out of that final door. Jakki and her mate Andrea were there. I threw my arms round Jakki, then Andrea. Dancing across the road, I went into the small corner shop – I knew it was there, I'd thought about this moment so much. I bought a bottle of Lucozade and walking home, looking at ordinary people, not screws or cons, I felt brilliant, and swore I'd never eat a plate of porridge again.

CHAPTER 9

About the Forty–Seven

ALMOST EXACTLY a year after the Ambush of Motherwell Casuals that saw forty seven arrests, I found out what these Casuals were doing then.

Steve, my cellmate in jail is living in London again and has a job as a storeman. Sutly is living with his parents and working on a drilling rig offshore.

Only one is married and he works as an engineer, he goes to watch the games now but not to fight, as does Sutly.

One of the boys did a three months' sentence for an assault charge a few weeks after the Ambush trial was over.

Three are presently on bail for allegedly trying to bring over £1000 worth of cannabis resin into Aberdeen.

Most are still working and jobs include: life support technician, male nurse, painter and decorator, accountant, baker, butcher, two joiners, an electrician, two students, van drivers, storemen, barmen, clothes shop assistants, and many more.

Including Steve, two no longer live in Aberdeen and a further eight have not been seen since the trial. At least one lad from the Bridge of Don, who gave incriminating evidence against me and Steve has not been able to go into the town for fear of a beating from Casuals. This has nothing to do with me, in fact after the trial, when I and seven others got three weeks for reports, I told him that I knew he was under pressure and only 16 and that I had no bad feeling towards him.

Left with 37, about 20 are active Casuals going to all the

decent away games where there is a good chance of a fight, the rest mainly just go to home games to watch the match, although still don't wear scarfs and keep up the fashion as well. Some still get involved but do it very carefully.

Well into the 1986/87 season now and the Aberdeen Soccer Casuals are still going strong, as are all the other crews. Already there have been battles, I heard there was a particularly good one at Parkhead. Is there then no stopping it?

I think that although the police can cut down trouble inside and around the ground, they will never stop the odd battles and they will never stop the hunger and the craving for violence and hooliganism.

CHAPTER 10

Why?

MOST PEOPLE'S attitude to the mobs is how to control them. More police everywhere, ban drink from football and from football buses and trains, ban away fans and have a members-only scheme. Certainly that is how the authorities think. I hope that I've shown here that the innocent bystander really has nothing to fear from the organised mobs.

But why do we do it in the first place? A lot of good-hearted people have tried to explain it as a result of modern society and to some extent that is right but there is a lot of stuff talked that is wrong and ignorant. Here are some of the mistakes.

One theory is that unemployment, depressing surroundings and poor prospects are reasons for the youth to rebel and turn to violence. No doubt that is true but that's nothing to do with the Casual scene from my knowledge and I have spoken to trendies from all over Britain. Out of the forty-seven Casuals arrested in the Motherwell ambush only five were out of work. Aberdeen is a beautiful clean city and has won the *Britain in Bloom* competition so often they had to ban us to encourage the others, so depressing surroundings cannot be considered as a factor to Aberdeen thugs. Nor can lack of prospects, for Aberdeen is the oil capital of Britain and prospects are very good indeed.

And parents can't be blamed in the case of soccer Casuals. Out of the forty seven only four came from homes where the parents were not still married and of those at least two were much loved by step parents. Most of the lads came from good homes with settled professional parents, had a good education with school trips abroad and all that sort of thing. I have had a very good upbringing, not spoiled, but well provided for, and my parents were quite strict about obedience. For the vast majority, I think it's fair to say the parents are blameless.

Drink plays a part, of course. Most of the lads like a drink before battle and some need it to help the nerves. But so do a lot of other people doing respectable things ... a night at the theatre would be a dry do without a drink at the interval. And it is a blunder to think drink motivates the Casuals. True some soccer violence wouldn't happen if it wasn't for drink. The mannie who is drunk when he thinks the ref gave a bad penalty against his team may go berserk and run on and kick the ref. Next morning he is sincere in court that he is ashamed of what he did which was done through drink. But the Casual isn't like that. He goes for the fight and never repents and no way can drink cause him to be violent.

Religious bigotry involving Protestants and Catholics certainly causes football troubles just as it causes trouble everywhere. It's mainly a feature of the Liverpool, Glasgow and Northern Irish teams wherever there is a drop of Irish blood thick enough to recall 1690. But doing away with football wouldn't stop the religious battles and an outbreak of peace among the Christians wouldn't stop the Casuals. Your religion can be a banner but you don't need it. After all you've got your team.

The same goes for Nazism which many have looked at for an explanation of the trendy phenomenon. Chelsea had a hard core of National Front supporters but they have subsided in the last few years. When we took a few car-loads down to see them play Newcastle at St James' Park we saw a few blacks in the Chelsea escort. Black players in England take a lot of stick but not particularly from trendies. Their colour is just an easy way to pinpoint a member of the opposition for a slagging rather than any real racial motive. Certainly most of the trendy violence is white on white and while there will always be echoes of what goes on elsewhere Nazism or any other -ism isn't what it's about at all.

A asked a lot of Casuals about all these theories and they mostly weren't very interested in the question. Most just don't have a clue. But I think my pal Ged spoke a lot of what we feel. He said "I'm so fed up with all the bullshit theories of why we ruck at football. I do it because I love it. I just love steaming into the away boys. It's magic. Fuck the theories. It's just magic fun."

It really shouldn't surprise anybody that so many of the youth today find that fun in violence. All our lives we have had the glories of the World Wars and the Vietnam War and even intergalactic war bombed at us by some of the greatest talents in the world. Films, magazines, comics and of course TV glorify battle with *Who Dares Wins* and *We'll Fight to the Death* . Try to think of how many films are aimed at the youth where the hero has to kill someone or batter someone somewhere along the line. In films like *Rollerball, Highlander, Warriors* and *The Wanderers* violence is drummed in and drummed in and it becomes so strong my stomach tightens up with excitement just writing this. How many heroes are gentle, mellow and peace-loving? *Ghandi* is the only one that I can think of.

And we really don't need all that encouragement for aggression is natural especially among males. Everyone does it. They compete at buying the best car or at the World Olympics. Look how millions participate in or spectate at violence in boxing, wrestling, karate, kung-fu, kick-boxing and many more and nothing excites the crowd more than when the sportsmen come to blows in ice hockey, Australian rules or grid-iron. Fighting is the ultimate competition with its danger and excitement.

My grandfather was in the Second World War and he used to talk about all that fighting that went on in Aberdeenshire before the First World War. He said there was so much death and destruction in that war and the next that the true horrors of war were apparent to everybody and that the desire to destroy physically had been satisfied. He lived to see the rise in mob violence in the 1970s and concluded that you need a war every twenty years to satisfy the natural aggression of the young. My generation didn't have a war so perhaps what we were doing was inventing our own. Maybe we are saying "Hey look, we can fight too."

There is a lot to lose though death is unlikely. You can lose the respect of relations, parents, and workmates. And friends who can't understand what you are doing will move on. You can lose skin off your face and be scarred for life as I am and, worst of all, you can go to jail as I did. So how can it be fun?

Most people can't understand how it could possibly be fun to be punched, booted and butted and to have bottles and stones thrown at you but believe me, I've experienced it, and when your in the thick of the action even sex doesn't come close to the feeling of being hyped-up so much. So what is it like?

I've never done it except on a mechanical one at Blackpool but I would imagine sitting on the back of a bull maddened by prickly straps around it at a rodeo and waiting for the gate to open would give you a similar thrill.

But I have got something of the same feeling from skiing. I love to ski and being at the top of a slope with ice and jumps on the way down can be like looking from the top of the terracing as you leave a soccer ground on a midweek game away from home with a small mob and a long way to go to the station.

I ski with no flair and no style but with a lot of determination. Being at the top of the terracing surveying the scene is similar to being at the top of a ski jump beyond your capabilities. Still I'd rather go for it even though I know there's virtually no chance of me not crashing. As I stand up with snow down my neck, a broken stick and start to get my skis back, I can at least feel the surge which comes from having dared.

Diving off the top board at the swimming baths is similar, Aberdeen's Bon Accord baths has the highest board in Scotland. Even the third board is a fearsome height and I've really hurt my head diving from there. The fourth is so high you may as well go right to the top. Up I went absolutely shiting myself with apprehension climbing the stairs from the third to the fifth. The heart thumps and the stomach is a turmoil of butterflies. I'd gone back but my brother John, the bastard, just went off so that was it. Standing on the edge the water looks no more than a garden pond. Will I even be able to hit it? There's only one way down but it's starting that is the problem. Shouts come up from below to hurry up. Something triggers me and we're off. "Holy shit!" The whole of my insides are in panicked nervous confusion. Then *batter* I hit the water and travel to the bottom of the

OFFICIAL NOTICE

SATURDAY 18th DECEMBER 1982
AT DUNDEE (JENS PARK)

NEXT SATURDAY WE TRAVAL to
DUNDEE AND WILL BE MET WITH
THE USUAL UNFRIENDLY ATMOSPHERE.
SO LETS PUT A STOP TO it BY
GOING TO DUNDEE IN FORCE BY
TRAIN. EVERYBODY WILL BE MEETING
IN THE ENCLOSURE END UNDER
THE STAND OPPOSITE THE CAMERA'S.
P.S.
NO SHITTERS. —
A!DEENTHUGS

ABERDEEN -v- HIBS

On 29th January we travel to Edinburgh to meet
Hibs in the Scottish Cup. After the match we
will have our usual battle with the Hibs fans.
The la᠉ c time we were there we showed them what
we thought of them. It was a day to be proud
of! Scum ran everywhere. We showed them that
Aberdeen fans fear no-one. They are a bunch of
mouths, just like Dundee Utd, Dundee, Hearts
and these mouths from Glasgow Rangers and
Celtic.

So lets go to Edinburgh in force by train. We
will catch the 9.55am train to Edinburgh. Don't
come if you are going to run - we only want
fighters. Fuck Hibs - Aberdeen Casuals Rule -
MUNICH HERE WE COME.

No Scarves,

No Kids,

No Runners.

sea. After I swim the half mile to the surface I punch the air.
Magic! I did it.

So being a Casual is great fun but as most people are against
us what can they do to stop it? Well there is no doubt that the
lack of involvement of the fans with the clubs in Britain is a
factor. In Spain, for example, they are kept up to date with all
the goings on at the clubs, join in functions, competitions and
meet the players. The Spanish clubs realise the importance of
the fans, involve them as much as possible and make them feel
a part of the club. In Britain the fiction writers on the back page
of the local papers is all you have to keep you going from one
Saturday to the next.

There is no doubt that organised hooliganism is partly the
fans way of getting involved in the goings on, of getting noticed
and of sharing the headlines with their heroes. A big story in the
press about your mob is a real boost to any Casual. Nothing
made us so proud as when the mob from little Aberdeen made
the main National news. If you have made the papers you have
had some kind of success.

I do think that involvement would help to reduce the violence but it can only make a small contribution unless it caters
for the need the Casuals have for physical violence. Why not
have a section of the ground set aside for battling? The police
would search for weapons on entry but otherwise let the
Casuals make their own rules. We would love that and no one
would be in that section unless they wanted to fight ... the
innocent would never be involved. If anything like that were
ever done I bet the people in the executive boxes would insist
that the Casual enclosure was right underneath their boxes so
they could have the best view of the action.

I can't leave this chapter without saying something about
the terrible events which will forever be associated with the
Heysel and Hillsborough stadiums. It should go without saying
that this is not what Casuals set out to achieve. These were
disasters which no Casual would want. But what is perhaps not
so obvious is that what happened there wasn't anything to do
with soccer Casual behaviour. I wasn't at either event but my
understanding was that they were caused by behaviour that is
against what Casuals are about.

At Hillsborough there were a lot of things that went wrong but the basic problem was a lot of genuine fans desperately excited not to miss a few seconds of football action and pushing and rushing as a consequence. The big event for the Casual is at the other end of the ground and normally has to wait till after the game.

And at Heysel the problem was caused by an attack on innocent Italian fans who had got tickets for the wrong end. Again there may have been some Casuals in that mad mob but it is no part of the Casuals behaviour to attack family fans and scarfers. The prize for the Casual is the trendy at the other end and, as the television clearly showed, his behaviour was every bit as bad as the Scouser's.

Glossary

Arches	Prison washing and slopping-out area
Bill	The Police
Blade	Knife used as an offensive weapon. In the football sense usually a Stanley knife. Frowned upon by true casuals.
Bonehead	Skinhead
Bounce	Typical casual reaction to a goal for the favoured team. The trendies jump up and down in unison while hugging and waving triumphal fists.
Boat	Face
Bum	Boast ... as in bum up your own City
Christmas Trees	Scarfers who wear as much club colour as they can. They may have scarves tied to their wrists and round their waists and wear club shirts as well.
Dour	Boring
Douts	Doups...cigarette ends which can be relit and as long as they are not cork tipped can be re-rolled to make new stronger smokes. Those re-rolls have a very high tar factor.
Fergie	Aberdeen's manager, subsequently with Manchester United
Huns	Rangers fans ... Protestants
Joint	Marijuana cigarette
Jumpers	Fare dodgers on the trains
Manny	Old fan, at least thirty. Goes to the football to watch the game and say everything isn't as good

as it used to be. Traditionally dressed in a flat cap, a coat and his scarf worn as a muffler.

Hash	Hashish...marijuana
Peter	Prison cell ... Rhyming slang from Peter Sellers
Pish	Urinate
Roll-ups	Roll your own cigarettes
Rubble	Rhyming slang...trouble, or a fight
Ruck	Fight involving more than two combatants
Runner	Doing a runner ... leaving (a restaurant) without paying
Scallies	From Scallywags. Soccer casuals especially from Liverpool
Scarfers	Football fans who, unlike the trendies, go to the football wearing scarves and jerseys showing which team they support
Score	Twenty pounds
Screw	Prison Officer Cheat as in screw the bandit ... steal from the fruit machine
Shot	Turn...It's my shot now
Skids	Underpants
Skinhead	Youth with stubble haircut and leathers, chains and other untrendy clothes
Shoot	Rhyming slang...shoot the craw...gang awa'. Disappear
Smoke	The...London
Tims	Celtic Fans ... Catholics
Trendies	Young men who are in fashion...after the fashion of the soccer casuals
Under Fives	Soccer casuals under the age at which they can readily pass for being old enough to drink in pubs
Tappers	Borrowers. From the mannies who come up and tap you on the shoulder and ask for a couple of bob for a cup of tea
Yids	Tottenham Hotspur fans ...their name not mine

AFC
"famous soccer hooligans"
CONGRATULATIONS:
YOU HAVE JUST MET THE
A/DEEN SOCCER CASUALS·
(SCOTLANDS' HARDEST)

Casual calling card

BLACK DIAMONDS
and the BLUE BRAZIL
Ron Ferguson's celebrated portrait
of Cowdenbeath and its team

"I thought when I read *Fever Pitch* by Nick Hornby, I had enjoyed the best book on football in recent times. I now know better: I found myself completely enthralled by *Black Diamonds and the Blue Brazil* which is absolutely superb... compelling reading. "

Craig Brown, Scottish football team manager

"Every now and again, perhaps once every five years, a book is published which captures the elusive essence of the game of football . . *Black Diamonds and the Blue Brazil* can stand comparison with the very best of football writing."

Scottish Football Historian

"Wondrous prose... bloody good, an object lesson in how to write a book on football... do yourself a favour and buy a copy."

The Absolute Game

Published by Famedram at £5.95 and available throughout Scotland, or by post from: PO Box 3, Ellon AB41 9EA